G000124316

Books by Matthew Lowes

Spirituality

That Which is Before You (2020)
When You are Silent It Speaks (2021)
A Billion Fingers Point at the Moon (Coming in 2022)

Fiction

The End of All Things (2018)

Games

Elements of Chess (2012)
Dungeon Solitaire: Labyrinth of Souls (2016)
Dungeon Solitaire: Devil's Playground (2018)

WHEN YOU ARE SILENT IT SPEAKS

WHEN
YOU ARE
SILENT
IT SPEAKS

MATTHEW LOWES

CHARTING THE SPIRITUAL PATH

Empty Press

2021

When You are Silent It Speaks:
Charting the Spiritual Path
/ Matthew Lowes
ISBN 978-1-952073-02-1 (pbk.)

Typeset in
Minion Pro by Robert Slimbach
Source Sans pro by Paul D. Hunt

Empty Press

matthewlowes.com

TABLE OF CONTENTS

The spiritual journey *is* your life,
exactly as it is.

Author's Note

The title of this book comes from the 40th verse in Yoka Daishi's *Song of Realizing the Way*.* It's worth reproducing here for its concise teaching. I first encountered these words in the lectures of Alan Watts, where they were recited with the following translation:

> You cannot take hold of it.
> You cannot get rid of it.
> In not being able to get it, you get it.
> When you are silent, it speaks.
> When you speak, it is silent.
> The great gate is wide open,
> And nobody obstructing it.

*A good translation and commentary on all 67 verses by the Venerable Myokyo-ni is available through The Buddhist Society.

ACKNOWLEDGEMENTS

Thanks to the true teacher, who takes many forms and appears in many guises to point out the way. Thanks to the students who help cultivate these teachings with their dedication to inquiry and practice. Thanks to all who guide and encourage those who are on the path.

Thanks to everyone who read various drafts of this book for their feedback, insights, and editing.

Special thanks to Joel Morwood, Kaizen Taki, Elizabeth Engstrom, Mark Hurwit, Alex Bronstein, Ryan Quitzow-James, Emily Bellinger, and Christina Lay.

Special thanks also to all my family and friends for their generous love and support.

WHEN YOU ARE SILENT IT SPEAKS

INTRODUCTION

This is the second book in a series addressing the topics of enlightenment, awakening, and the spiritual path. May it aid you on your journey, and may it be of some use in bringing illumination, true happiness, and an end to suffering.

Each book stands on its own, but the series is perhaps best approached in order. The first book, *That Which is Before You,* includes an account of my awakening and an overview of insights, teachings, and practices. *When You are Silent It Speaks* is dedicated to a more detailed discussion of the spiritual journey. The topics in this book were selected and organized to explore stages along the spiritual path — beginning, middle, and end.

Note that although I freely use examples and adopt vocabulary from various traditions, I am not an expert on religions and I claim no authority other than direct insight and experience. It is not my intention to support or challenge any particular tradition or religion, or for that matter any process or theory of science. The essence of the teaching is universal. It speaks to all people, of all times, of all faiths, and of no faith.

These discourses can serve as a map for the spiritual journey that is shared by all. Take note, however, that it is more a topographical map than a road map. As J. Krishnamurti put it, "truth is a pathless land," so following this pathless path is not as simple as believing such and such or doing a, b, and c … or for that matter, not doing x, y, and z.

You will still need a compass, and you will need your wits about you to navigate. You will need to note landmarks, recognize the tracks of animals, follow the passage of the sun and moon, and mark the orientation of the stars. You will need to build your own fire, but do not fear — the spark is already present, and hopefully this map can reveal a bit of the terrain. It may suggest routes, reveal obstacles, and point toward sources of good food and clean water to sustain you along the way.

PART I

THE SITUATION

1

SPIRITUAL ADVENTURE

*The spiritual journey is not something separate
from your life; it is your life, exactly as it is.*

THE STRUGGLES OF LIFE

Behind the everyday struggles of life — to secure shelter, find food, reproduce, care for children, and so on — there is another struggle going on. It may linger way in the back of your mind, or it may have worked its way into the forefront of your awareness. But on some level, we're all aware of it. Something seems not quite right about our situation. Something seems missing. And we intuitively feel that what's *really* happening and what we think is happening are not exactly the same.

We can never quite put our finger on what it is, nor definitively identify what's missing. Nevertheless, the mind seeks understanding, and so we end up accounting for it in various ways. Frequently, we attribute it to some fulfillment we might gain in the future, through a job, a relationship, a family, a personal goal, an identity, a purpose, or any number of various things. We may also attribute it to something lost, such as a loved one, our youth, our innocence, our dreams, or our purpose. We may attribute it to some defect in ourselves, our history, or the world, some mental or emotional instability, some past trauma, or some political circumstance. We may attribute it to something metaphysical, religious, or spiritual in the form of a distant god, a heaven to come, a lost paradise, or an unseen spiritual realm or power. We may attribute it to some lack of sufficient knowledge, and so on.

In reality, we employ all these strategies and more. We are constantly cooking the books to account for this thing. We are always shifting something around to cover this mysterious lack, and we hope nobody will notice, especially ourselves. For this thing seems like a kind of black hole at the center of our being, and if we looked at it, if we really acknowledged it as it is, it would swallow us up. And that's a terrifying prospect. Better to assume it is something other than that. Better to keep busy. Better to keep looking elsewhere. Maybe if we improved ourselves or our situation enough, that thing at the back of our minds would just go away, or reveal itself to be something other than a terrifying black hole.

In some sense, we end up ignoring the very thing we are missing, because we don't like the look of it from afar. We much prefer the apparent safety of our existing ideas and beliefs. And whatever kind of world we live in, so much of our activity in life comes by way of trying to keep up that world's pretenses. We cling to our ideas, pursue our endeavors, and continue searching, so that we can put off gazing directly into the unknown.

So what is this struggle that is going on behind the everyday struggles of life? Strangely, it is a struggle both to find what is missing … and to ignore it. What is missing is actually always present, but by ignoring it we continue searching, and through searching we continue ignoring. It's a kind of feedback loop that is maintained by not letting the right hand know what the left hand is doing. Seen in this light, it's no wonder we're confused, conflicted, and ill at ease. It's no wonder we feel alienated, unfulfilled, and at odds with ourselves and the world.

The highest form of this search and its ultimate manifestation, from the very beginning, is the search to see through our ignorance and gaze directly into the emptiness at the center of our being, to see beyond it, and thus put an end to the search altogether. This is nothing other than the quest for enlightenment. It is the search for the Self, for Truth, for God, and for liberation in this life.

And so, in the end, all the struggles of one's life, whatever name they go by, and whether they seem spiritual or not, can be seen as a part of this one great quest.

THE SPIRIT WORLD

Where can we begin when there is no beginning or end? Perhaps we can begin with an acknowledgement that we are all in this together. There are as many paths and approaches as there are people, but ultimately the spiritual quest is the same for us all. There are many kinds of particular difficulties and delusions to see through, but the journey encompasses all ideas, all beliefs, all concepts, all worlds, all views. And its end is not an image or a model of the truth, couched in cultural, religious, or even scientific metaphor, but truth itself, which cannot, by its nature, be described, modeled, or conceptualized.

In this sense, all paths lead to the truth. Even paths that seem to avoid the truth lead to the truth. For if followed, eventually the unreal, the untrue, and the impermanent must, by their very nature, collapse. Thus, all ideas are incomplete, all concepts are doomed, all metaphors are flawed, all views are wrong. And so the scientist and the religious devotee are, in some sense, in the same boat. The atheist and the true believer have more in common than they realize. All discreet views fail to grasp the absolute truth itself. This acknowledgement should at least engender some worldly compassion. Though we may disagree about how to approach it, we are all in the same basic situation.

Practically speaking, however, when we attempt to directly ascertain the substance and nature of the truth, we are talking about a spiritual path. Working to attain intimate knowledge of the ultimate reality is traditionally thought of as a spiritual endeavor, so that is the focus here. Nevertheless, language is incredibly tricky. Just by calling it a spiritual path, some people may already be led astray. So perhaps we should also make an effort to discuss just what we mean by *spiritual* in this context.

By referring to a spiritual path, I do not necessarily mean a religious path. Nor does it necessarily have anything to do with ghosts, angels, or supernatural beings. Nor is it a singular or particular path. Nor is it ultimately a path at all. That is just a metaphor. *Spiritual* in this context means seeking for or attaining to the ultimate truth. And the first step on such a path is simply to recognize that we do not know what the truth is. When we sense our fundamental ignorance about what is really happening, we have already stepped out upon the pathless path.

Spirit, then, is not some substance, nor some insubstantial force. Spirit is what's real and true, beyond all our ideas, conceptions, and metaphors, whether we know it or not. While we are ignorant of it, spirit is the pure unknown. It's like the variable in a complex algebraic equation. But while the equation may look good — impressive and intricate and beautiful — too often we mistake the equation itself for the solution.

To illustrate this point further, I would like say that spirit is not something other than the mind, or the body, or the physical world. We may think we know what these things are, and so assume that spirit must be something else. For example, we may think, *I am my mind and this body, existing in a physical world.* We may imagine we have a pretty good idea what we're talking about. In fact, we may have a whole host of ideas and beliefs about what the mind is, what the body is, and what the physical world is. But when we really examine these ideas and beliefs carefully, we find that they are all founded upon other ideas and beliefs, and when we get right down to it, we don't know what these things are. The whole idea that we do is an illusion. We don't know what the mind is. We don't know what the body is. And the physical world? It's just an idea, a phrase we came up with to refer to certain aspects of our experience. But on the most fundamental level, we do not know. We do not know what matter is, or space. How can we know what the physical world is?

And so, when we do *not* know, with utter clarity, we may realize that *this* is the spirit world. It is not elsewhere. We are already in it. Everything that is happening is a movement of this spirit. All actions are spiritual in nature, and every path is a spiritual path.

THE ORIGINS OF RELIGION

Long before recorded history, human beings huddled around the light of fires, under starry skies, in deep forests, and in the shelter of caves to tell their stories. Imagine the kinds of raw experiences they had. Imagine the stories they must have told. People knew little or nothing of what lay beyond the horizon. And at night, in the darkness, that circle of knowledge shrank to the dim glow of a campfire, if they were lucky enough to have one. The stars were a mystery, animals were otherworldly, and death was a great enigma. There, among our ancestors, the great archetypal myths were born.

Of course, everything changes, but the basic situation we are in has not changed as much as we like to think. We are still confronted with the mysteries of experience, the struggles of life, and the enigma of death. And no matter how vast our worldly knowledge, our ability to explain, and no matter how complex our conceptual understanding or how detailed our model of the universe, there is always a horizon, a limit to the light of our meager campfire, beyond which lies a direct confrontation with the unknown.

The concept of religion itself, as discreet and mutually exclusive collections of beliefs, appears to be a fairly recent development. As recently as a few hundred years ago, nobody thought about religion this way, nor was there really a word for religion in this sense. But human beings have always been filled with wonder and awe, and have always sought answers to the mysteries of experience and the difficulties of life. So the kinds of ideas, teachings, and practices that make up religions have been around from the beginning.

We tend to lump all these ideas into the same religious category, but there are actually two distinct strands that comprise the origins of religious thought. And although one may spring from the other, some examination of how they differ could prove insightful.

On the one hand, there are the outward forms, which come to us as names, images, stories, assertions, rituals, practices, and so on. These forms are deeply imaginative, wonderfully evocative, and richly metaphorical. At this level, all the differences between beliefs and the great diversity of religions and practices are manifested. But these forms are also, by their nature, bound and shaped by the limitations of language, image, and culture. Locked into the viewpoint of this level, without acknowledgement of such limitations, all the disputes, arguments, and conflicts between religions also become manifested. And all the abuses of dogmatic belief arise from the ignorance of delusion.

On the other hand, most religions also have have an inward mystical tradition that points toward a fundamental, experiential, direct knowledge of limitless reality and truth as both the origin and ultimate end of all outward forms. At this level, there can be no conflict. Distinctions between religious ideas and practices, concepts and beliefs, are in form only. And all forms, including all religious forms, lead back to the same transcendent reality. It cannot be otherwise.

While many religious ideas have spread through imaginative stories, images, and explanations, it seems likely that all religious traditions, if traced back far enough, have in their roots a direct realization of this one reality and truth. But this truth, being without any limitation or division, is ineffable. It cannot be conveyed in words or images. Thus, it cannot really be passed on in the way a story, a picture, a map, or an explanation can be passed on. One must really come to it and realize for oneself that which is beyond all stories, all pictures, all maps, all explanations, all concepts, all thoughts, all words.

So while many religious traditions seem to point toward a story, an image, an explanation, a theology, or a cosmology, and say "Believe this," the inner, mystical, and sometimes secret teachings point toward the ineffable, and say "Find out for yourself."

Sin, Psychology,
and the Wheel of Samsara

If a person sets out to discover and know the truth, immediately questions arise: *In which direction do I go? How shall I proceed?* And while ultimately the truth is ever present and inescapable, realizing it is another matter. At the beginning, some direction — or at least some kind of orientation — may be helpful.

Without proposing that any particular model of the universe is correct or incorrect, much can be learned about the landscape of the spirit by an examination of various models that have arisen. By treating these models as clues rather than definitive explanations, as pointing toward rather than being the truth, we might try to orient ourselves with regard to our search. To this end, let us discuss the matters of sin, psychology, and the wheel of samsara, three different ideas that reflect a common underlying structure in their most basic forms.

Many people cringe at the very notion of sin from having grown up in a particular type of religious environment. They are shackled to the idea of sin as transgression against a divine law, even to the point of defining it with written rules. But this is a rather simplistic interpretation. Any written rules are merely outward forms, limited by language and culture, attempting to reflect or approximate a deeper truth. The idea of a divine law is metaphorical, so sin as a kind of supernatural crime is also metaphorical, at best.

To understand sin from a different perspective, let's just look at what it supposedly does. Forget about what exactly constitutes a sin. What happens when a person is sinful? That's a more interesting question. Clearly, sin has the supposed effect of separating one's soul from God and from paradise. So a basic definition of sin could be: thoughts and actions that separate one from God. Forget about the specifics for now, and let's just establish that if we are searching for God, somehow our own thoughts and actions could be an issue.

In the modern era, care of the soul has given way to the care of the mind and the study of the psyche. The search for God has given way to the search for happiness, and this brings us to psychology. Interestingly, the word *psyche* originally meant "soul." So in some sense, we have just shifted our terms around and changed our explanations while confronting or avoiding the same basic issues. In this way of thinking, sin has been recast as aberrant, unwanted, or problematic mental activity or behavior.

Human states of mind range from ecstatically blissful to truly horrific. We're all over the map, but there is a general feeling that people want to avoid what we judge as bad states — anxiety, fear, anger — and move toward what we judge as good states — happiness, love, fulfillment. On a basic level, psychology is engaged with the study of the mind, mental activity, and behavior in order to help us move toward good states, as individuals and as a larger society. Underlying that notion is, again, the idea that somehow our own thoughts and actions keep us from the object of our search — in this case, happiness.

Samsara is a cycle of birth and death to which one is bound by karma in the form of causative thoughts and actions. Unlike sin, karma can be good or bad, causing either good effects and a better incarnation or bad effect and a worse incarnation. But as long as one continues to create karma, good or bad, they are bound to be born and die again, and are destined to suffer. Because of the cyclical and unending nature of samsara, what goes up, must eventually come down.

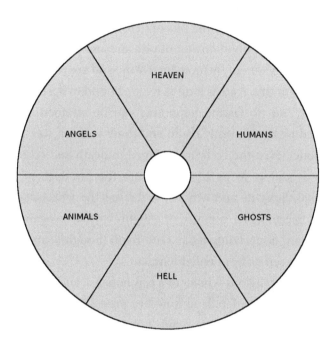

The various possible incarnations in samsara can be mapped out into various realms on a wheel. At the top of the wheel is heaven, the realm of heavenly gods. To the left is something like an angelic realm, or a realm of jealous gods and semi-divine beings. To the right is the human realm. Below the angelic realm is the animal realm, and below the human realm is a ghost realm, where hungry spirits are tormented by insatiable desires that can never be fulfilled. At the bottom of the wheel is the hell realm — no explanation needed there.

The wheel of samsara can be imagined as a grand metaphysical model of the universe, but it can also be understood as a map of human psychological states. Sometimes we are up in the realm of the gods, other times in the pits of hell, but we are always bound to this cycle of ups and downs, of pleasure and pain, of happiness and despair. Moment by moment, we die and are reborn onto the wheel of samsara. And as long as we are bound to it, suffering will reappear and no lasting happiness can be attained. Don't be confused by the heavenly realm and think you can stay there. In this model, even the gods are doomed to death and rebirth. The only way out is to be liberated from the bondage of karma, causative thoughts and actions, and from the wheel itself. This liberation is moksha, nirvana, or enlightenment. So again, we can discern an underlying idea. Our own thoughts and actions somehow keep us from enlightenment.

I'm not a religious scholar or a psychologist, and I know people can pick apart the details of how I've presented these ideas, but that would be missing the point. I'm not advocating for any of these views. They are only views. They are only ideas. Our interest here is in orienting ourselves for a spiritual search. The ideas are presented in order to illuminate a common thread with regard to this search. In each case, the desired thing is separated from us by our own thoughts and actions. The thread suggests that God, happiness, and enlightenment are all one truth, and that somehow our own thoughts and actions cut us off from it.

This is a clue, suggesting that to continue this search, we might look inward. We might try to somehow fundamentally confront ourselves. We might seek to find out who is thinking these thoughts, and who is taking these actions. What is the origin of these thoughts and actions? And in this way, we might seek to find out who or what we really are.

THE GREAT ADVENTURE

There are many types of stories: romance, journey, comedy, tragedy, horror, quest, and so on. We can find examples of these in myths from just about every culture and era. And these archetypal stories are mirrored in the stories people tell about themselves, others, and everyday life. Not everyone reaches the fantastical heights of the great myths, but all the elements are there. We are storytellers at heart, not just when it comes to myth making, but in our everyday existence — minute to minute, hour to hour, year to year.

From birth to death, our lives are a collection of stories we tell about ourselves, full of journeys and quests, comedies and tragedies. But is this actually what life is — a collection of stories about imagined events — or is there something else going on?

Apart from these stories about the past and future, what is the raw experience we are having, right now?

When all our personal stories — or enough of them — have run their course, questions may begin to arise about what's really happening. Sometimes the questions are explicitly articulated: *What is the purpose of my life? Why do I keep suffering? How can I get out of this? What's wrong with me? Is there anything else?* Other times they may rumble beneath the surface of articulation, manifesting as a growing discontent with a seemingly intolerable and unsolvable problem. And somehow, although we can't quite figure how, that problem is our self.

These questions lead right to the heart of a great existential mystery. They steer us toward that black hole at the center of our being, the one we have tried to ignore, the one we tried to cover up with all the stories — layer upon layer upon layer. And we may wonder: *If I am not this collection of stories, these thoughts and memories and dreams, what am I? Who is creating these stories? Who is the thinker? Who is the rememberer? Who is the dreamer?*

A kind of meta-narrative begins to take shape, that aims at finding out the truth behind all these stories. This is the great adventure, encompassing all the types of stories and ways of looking at our lives. It takes many forms. As a romance, it is a falling in love. As a journey, it is a journey home. As a comedy, it is a comedy of errors, of misunderstandings and mistaken identities. As a tragedy, it is the consequence of our thoughts and actions. As a horror, it is a confrontation with the unknown and with our deepest, most troubling fears. As a quest, it is the ultimate quest, the search for truth and realization. In all its forms, it is a narrative of desire, suffering, disillusionment, discovery, and transformation.

In practice, all stories may contain elements from the various types of stories, and each story can be interpreted from a multitude of perspectives. But every story has at least one character, and all characters want something. If they didn't want something, there would be no story, no conflict or tension with the situation as it is. Since all characters want something, are seeking something, all stories contain an element of the quintessential quest.

The objects of desire may change, but all quests eventually lead to further quests, because nothing grants lasting satisfaction. It may take a few story cycles to figure this out — a few times around the wheel of samsara — but there is no way to escape it. In this manner, sooner or later, we begin to understand that what we're really looking for is that truth which lies beyond all stories, at the very heart of our being. It is the ultimate quest to solve the enigma of the spirit, to find and face the unknown.

The good news is that you don't have to load up your ships and set sail for a far-off land. You don't even have to pack your bags to go on this ultimate quest. You are already on it! This great spiritual adventure is not something separate from your life and the path you've taken so far. It *is* your life, exactly as it is.

2

THE NOISE OF DELUSION

Nothing is simpler than the truth,
but nothing is more confusing than our ideas about it.

THE NATURE OF IGNORANCE

A fish, they say, does not know the water, and does not consider the abyssal depths. A bird in flight does not know the air, and does not think twice about the soaring heights. Like this, human beings are ignorant of the reality in which they exist, and do not realize that which is ever present. It's not a matter of stupidity or a lack of information. It's just the fundamental situation we find ourselves in. The reality is always there … and partly because it is always there, we are conditioned to ignore it.

All things are intelligible through contrast. We understand light through dark, up through down, good through evil, inside through outside. We see objects because they appear in space, and because they stand out against a contrasting background. We hear noise by virtue of the silence in which sounds arise. This is the nature of all things. All things depend on other things. But when we think about things, we always leave something out. When we think about the light, we ignore the darkness in which it must appear. By embracing the good, we ignore its dependence on evil. By focusing outward, we ignore its relation to the depths of our interior.

All such dualities are really two sides of a unified oneness. But by leaving something out, by always ignoring some aspect of this whole, we lose sight of the ultimate, undifferentiated reality. And this is only the surface of our ignorance. By ignoring things — by leaving things out — we set in motion a whole chain reaction of misunderstandings and misapprehensions, of confabulations and beliefs, which completely obscure the apprehension of the ever-present reality itself.

By naming things and assigning limits and attributes to them, we create an abstraction of experience. Based in part on various perceptions of contrast, we break the world up into discreet objects and events. But again, we always leave something out. In this case, we forget that we are the creator of names, the assigner of limits and attributes. While ignoring this, we tend to mistake our abstractions, our ideas of things, for a permanent, abiding reality, thus further occluding the fundamental reality that lies beyond names and ideas, beyond objects and events.

Once we've populated the world with a multitude of things, we begin to think about them. We ponder their relationships. We speculate on their origins, compositions, and behaviors. In short, we construct a conceptual understanding of the world we have created. We begin to explain things. And although our explanations may make sense of events and objects, empowering us with a kind of functional knowledge, the explanations add yet another layer of thought, obscuring the fundamental reality we ignored at the beginning.

At each stage of our ignorance, with each layer of thought covering the ultimate reality, the obscurations we create are solidified through belief. This is not the kind of belief in which you might choose one god, idea, or explanation over another, but a more fundamental belief — a belief in distinctions and explanations in general. It is a kind of belief over which you have little or no control. So, with each thing we mistakenly take as true, whatever it may be, the world we create seems more solid and real. With regard to absolute truth, however, this world and the beings that inhabit it have been built up upon a series of delusions.

The state of ignorance, based on ignoring some aspect of what is happening, is perpetuated through a cycle of delusions and beliefs. Our functional explanations, although workable, only confirm what are fundamentally misapprehensions with regard to the ultimate truth. But behind it all, there *is* a shining unassailable truth which we have forgotten, which we have covered up, which we have hidden and made secret, even from ourselves. Although one may be ignorant of it, it is common to all things, always with us, ever present, eternally here and now.

Maybe this all sounds strange, doubtful, or highly theoretical. After all, a chair is a chair, a tree is a tree, and it's obvious that we are living in this world of things and events, of vast histories, of planets and stars and galaxies. But remember, there's something we're leaving out …

We are like fish in water.

We are like birds in air.

BELIEF AND CONFABULATION

Until belief itself is transcended, all are subjected to it. As long as we are in a state of ignorance, trapped within the cycle of samsaric delusion, some trace of belief will remain, in part because we believe in the obscurations of our thoughts, and in part because we do not know what lies beyond our thoughts and beliefs. Again, this is just the basic situation we find ourselves in. There is no judgment attached to it.

Whatever our beliefs — be they conscious or unconscious — they are the framework for the stories we tell about ourselves and the world. Of course, the stories themselves become the objects of belief, and thus are incorporated into the cycle of delusion. Layer upon layer, they distract us from the essential truth that we have hidden from ourselves.

The stories are endless and unfold with kaleidoscopic and mind-boggling diversity. Imagine the sheer number of human beings in the world, and that each person is carrying around their own collection of stories with a unique perspective, unique circumstances, and a unique stream of thoughts, emotions, and sensations. In this way, each person, each point of view, can be seen as an entire worldview.

We are usually under the impression that our point of view — our memories, sensations, emotions, and thoughts — represents at least a fairly accurate experience of an external world and the bodies in which we seem to exist. But is this really the case? Or is it possible that we are fooled or misled in some way that we are unaware of? If we are interested in discovering the truth, this is worth considering.

In fact, there are many examples in everyday experience in which it's quite clear that we are easily deceived. Take dreams, for instance. In the midst of a dream, usually we don't think we are dreaming. Although that's possible, usually we take the dream at face value … until we wake up. Similarly, memories of a single event can prove wildly diverse and inaccurate. The senses can be fooled with a wide variety of illusions, or co-opted by hallucinations. And we may become disillusioned with even strongly-held beliefs. Afterward, we may come to view our previously-held ideas as mistaken or even foolish. But no matter how many times we are fooled by such circumstances, we continue to believe there *is* a right view. And yet it is ever so hard to pin down.

What if, however, these examples are clues to a deeper truth? What if there is no right view? What if all the stories we tell ourselves about what is happening, from the most metaphysical to the most mundane, are a confabulation based on subtly and not-so-subtly held beliefs? Deep down, we already feel we are missing something, that we are separated from something. Could this be what it is? What is the view of *no-view?* How can we even make sense of that?

Taking nothing for granted, memory itself is unverifiable. By virtue of a memory, we may feel that such and such has happened, but all we really know is the present memory. We actually do not know anything about the past, or even if it exists. The past is a confabulation based in part on a belief that the past is something real. This may seem extreme. I've been trying to suggest more than state here, but the direction of this discourse is quite radical. It does not lead to the kind of understanding attainable through a view. The view of no-view is quite bewildering.

If we just consider the possibility that our lives and our world could be a kind of grand confabulation, a collection of stories based on beliefs, we may then go on to question all the beliefs we hold. In doing so, we would have to confront the possibility that many of the ideas we take for granted as real, even some very basic presuppositions, are more along the lines of deeply-held beliefs.

So then, what do you believe?

This is a much deeper question than it may seem at the outset — much, much deeper.

What lies beyond belief?

The answer is closer to you than your own skin. It is closer than your thoughts. It is closer than anything you can imagine.

THE VEIL OF MAGIC

Reported sayings from the world's spiritual literature all hint at a hidden reality, beyond our ordinary conceptions of the world. Jesus said "The kingdom of heaven is spread upon the earth, yet people do not see it." When the Buddha was asked what he was, god or man, he simply said "I am awake," implying that the ordinary person is somehow asleep. And Lord Krishna said "Only one in a thousand would truly seek him, and only one in a thousand who seek, would see him as he is."

These are just examples from some well-known spiritual literature. I shared these ones because I'm familiar with them, but similar sayings are found throughout many texts and traditions, all suggesting there is something we do not know. What does it all mean? Were the original writers just making stuff up, or does an esoteric meaning point to a hidden truth we have yet to realize? If there *is* something hidden — and indeed our intuition suggests that there is — where could it possibly be and what stands in the way of seeing it?

Religious traditions present us with a variety of metaphors for this hidden reality: a spirit realm, a kingdom of God, a waking world, or truth itself. In the Christian tradition, it seems we are afflicted with a kind of blindness, until by grace we see. In the Buddhist tradition, it seems we are asleep, until somehow we awaken. In the Hindu and Buddhist traditions, there is a veil called *maya* that separates us from truth and liberation.

Maya is a Sanskrit word with a variety of nuanced and debated meanings. It is most often translated as "illusion," but can also be interpreted as "magic," "appearance," or "power." However it is translated, it seems to be understood as something which obscures the true nature of reality. With the power of maya, the whole phenomenal world appears, but we misidentify ourselves and become deluded about the nature of objects and events, thoughts and sensations, time and space, life and death. We do not see things as they are, but rather as we think and believe them to be.

It's hard to imagine this while we're wrapped up in it. It's hard to fathom how we could be so fundamentally mistaken about what is happening — in fact, what is right before our eyes. We don't want to think about ourselves as deluded, but that too is just a way of looking at things. This power of illusion is what grants life all its excitement and drama, its gripping suspense and marvelous diversity of activity and ideas. But it is also, in its way, the source all suffering, seeking, loneliness, separation, and despair.

It's only natural that one might seek to lift this veil, to go beyond it, and see for oneself this kingdom of heaven that is revealed. However, being entirely wrapped up in it, we are hard pressed to find a way. If what we are experiencing is somehow like a dream, we do not know how to wake up from it.

Perhaps, at least, we can consider what this veil is made of. It is woven of thread spun from words and metaphors, ideas and concepts, thoughts and measurements, stories and judgments. And above all else, it is made whole through desire.

Self, Other, Mind, Body, and World

How do we make sense of what's happening? Generally, we do this by dividing it up, by breaking it into pieces and making distinctions between them. We describe these pieces by assigning them limits and attributes. We name them and define their relationships to other pieces. Some pieces we identify with and some we consider foreign, some we like and some we dislike, some we hope for and some we fear.

One of the primary distinctions we make, if not *the* primary distinction, is the distinction between self and other. Various phenomena are categorized as voluntary or involuntary, interior or exterior, thought or not thought, subject or object. The former of all these we combine together to form an idea of a self, and the later we combine to form the other or the world — everything that is not a part of the individual self. And into these two categories, we divide all phenomena.

Through this process, we conceptualize and identify with a body. We associate its various structures and processes with our idea of a self. And we attribute to it a past and a future, a birth and a death, which we identify as the past and future self.

Along the way, with our thoughts, emotions, and sensations, we conceptualize a kind of incorporeal entity which we further identify with. We think of this as our mind or our ego. And to it we continue to attach all the various phenomena that we categorize as self.

Out of everything that is other, we create and subdivide an entire world, from the images that are right before our eyes to the farthest reaches of the universe. We fill this world with the vastness of space and time. And we populate it with innumerable objects, events, and interactions.

That's it, that's everything ... or is it? New divisions, new events, new objects, and new interactions are constantly arising. But by now, the die is cast. As each thing arises, we think we are discovering new things about ourselves or the world, and we go on trying to make sense of it all.

Some things we think about as both self and other, depending on circumstances. The body, for instance, we think about as being our body when we have voluntary control over some aspect of its actions. When we don't, such as when it ages or dies, we think about it more as an object that is external to us. But we do not doubt the validity of our distinctions and categories. Nor do we doubt the reality of the ego-self, nor of the world or any of the objects in it.

Somewhere along the line we forgot our involvement in this whole process. We no longer see clearly how everything arises. And it is then that the ego-self and the broken-up world we have created becomes the noise of delusion, the veil of maya. Ultimately, in order to make some sense of anything, we end up ignoring the essential unity of the indivisible whole. That is the one thing we can't make sense of.

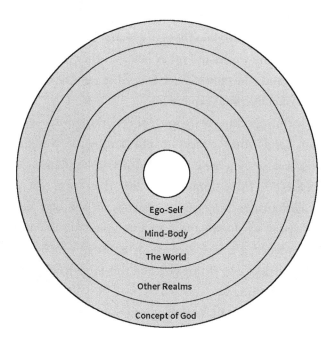

Conceptual Experience

While we are bound to the wheel of samsara and wrapped up in delusions of self and other — ego, mind, body, and world — the experience we are having is a thought-created, conceptual experience. It is as if we are hypnotized by the powerful magic of maya, caught in a web of illusions and appearances. It is as if we are dreaming. We do not know we are dreaming, and we cannot wake up from our dream.

For the purposes of illustration, we can map this dream onto a disk with a hole in the center. Here the disk contains concentric rings, with each ring representing an area of conceptualization. The inner two rings contain the ego-self and mind-body. The outer rings contain the world and other beings, other imagined realms and beings, and concepts of God. Everything on the disk is within the realm of conceptual experience.

In forming concepts, we collect thoughts, sensations, emotions, and other concepts into a kind of conglomerate, metaphorical, or aggregate idea. In order to hold any weight, all concepts rest on these things. These things, in turn, rest on other things. Perhaps, as they say, it's turtles all the way down. Or perhaps we can see the situation as a spontaneously arising, mutual interdependence, a kind tensegrity structure in which everything is held together by everything else. But this too is a concept. Could it all rest on nothing?

Whatever beliefs, ideas, and concepts we hold, they shape our experience, and through them we interpret whatever arises. The task of dividing and categorizing, naming and making sense of things, never ends. As long as we keep searching for answers, it will be an ongoing and infinite search. And as long as we cling to our concepts, we will never see beyond them. The trouble is, of course, how to know what we are clinging to. Some ideas, usually the tenuous ones, are obvious, but others are so deeply rooted that they are experienced as absolutely real. How do we get beyond that?

The deepest held concept is none other than the individual self, the ego. With this self comes thoughts and emotions, sensations and actions, birth and death, and so on. But what is the substance of the ego, if not this collection of disparate and fleeting things? What is the ego-self? Is it not just an idea we have about who we are, a pattern of thoughts and memories, and a collection of stories surrounding them?

The physical world itself, that paragon of concrete believability, is itself just an idea — a metaphor for that which is beyond our understanding. It is just a name we've given to what is happening. But on the most fundamental level, we do not know what matter is, nor space, nor time. We call it the physical world, but we don't really know what we are saying when we say that. When we conceptualize it as a material, mechanistic phenomenon, and believe wholeheartedly in the reality of this conceptualized view, that is how we experience it.

This is what I mean by conceptual experience.

What exists is beyond all ideas, beyond all concepts. But as long as we remain wrapped in the opacity of thought, we cannot realize it. In the disk illustration, to go beyond concepts, we must venture beyond the inner or outer boundary of the disk. There we may suddenly see the paper upon which the diagram is drawn, and realize that inside (True Self), outside (God), and everything in-between are united in sameness.

3

THE BEGINNING OF INQUIRY

Before we even know the question, we are searching for answers.

WHAT IS REALLY HAPPENING?

Who am I? Where did I come from? Why am I here? How do I find happiness? Is there a God? What happens after death?

Questions like these arise because we are already searching for answers. They arise in the context of separation. We already feel something is missing and desire to find it. Otherwise, no question would arise. As long as the questions *have* arisen, though, and continue to arise, perhaps we should endeavor to inquire further. Why not see where they lead? After all, any one of them may lead to the truth.

This is the beginning of spiritual inquiry. But we should be clear at the outset, that we must cast aside all conceptual answers that arise in the mind, the simple ones as well as the complex ones.

We are not looking for any kind of explanation. We are looking for clear insight. A mind conditioned to conceptual experience may have a difficult time even understanding what this means, but nevertheless this is what we must strive for.

In this endeavor, don't allow yourself any easy way out. We should not accept any conditioned answer that arises in the mind. Nor should we accept anyone else's explanation for how things are and what we're doing here. These are not easy questions. And if we have in mind that we will somehow solve them by the addition of a new explanation, or by adding up existing explanations, or by any kind of addition whatsoever, we've got the wrong idea about the goals of this inquiry.

Of course, you should try to see things in new ways, but only in order to dismantle the old ways. Clinging to any idea, new or old, will continue the cycle of delusion and ignorance. If you believe in a self, it may be helpful to really consider no-self. If you believe in no-self, it may be helpful to really consider the universal Self. If you believe in God, consider the absence of the God you believe in. If you don't believe in God, consider the eternal presence of what you might call God. And so on. But do not flip-flop and latch on to new beliefs. See things differently as a way of deconstructing beliefs all together.

This kind of inquiry is a process of discovering and discarding the unreal and the untrue, including all transitory ideas, thoughts, beliefs, desires, and concepts. Recognize these things for what they are — just ideas, thoughts, beliefs, and so on. They are not knowledge of the truth itself.

After some attempts to discard these things, you may be left to wonder: *What else is there?* Now you may be getting somewhere. Don't abandon your inquiry. Get right down to the bottom of it, and ask yourself: *What can I really say for certain?* It's a devastating question. Following it to the end may put you in direct contact with the unknown. And when the mind stops, that is when to really pay attention.

CONTEMPLATING IDENTITY

The revered sage Ramana Maharshi advised self-inquiry as the most direct path to realization. He recommended asking the question "Who am I?" and to seek internally the source of the "I-thought" without ceasing. Although Ramana did not always recommend this to people who were already pursuing other practices, there's a good case to be made for it. For whatever path one takes, this prime existential question must ultimately be addressed. Why not address it from the very beginning?

As long as this question of identity remains, as long as there is some doubt about who or what we really are, separation will persist. The question itself is a manifestation of duality. And because there is nothing more personal or important to us than this I-thought, this question goes right to the heart of the matter. To ask *Who am I? What am I? Do I exist?* or some other such fundamental question of identity is to question everything, for all our conceptual experience is experienced through this I-thought.

The apparent simplicity of the question, along with the inadequacy of any mentally formulated answer, is part of its strength. If taken seriously, all the difficulties and traps of inquiry are immediately on display, for it is clear that the purpose of the question is not to elicit an answer. It will not do to say, "I'm Joe Blow" or "I'm the son of John and Susan Blow" or "I'm this mind and body," or "I'm a person" or "I'm a human being," or even "I'm a soul" or "I'm this universe," or any other answer rooted in a name, a relationship, or a concept. When this is clear, the mental faculties are left dumbfounded.

When the mind cannot form or reach a satisfactory answer, when each attempt to really find this "I" fails, we may feel as if we have reached the end of the inquiry. But actually, that is just the beginning. All mentally formulated answers have to be exhausted. No satisfactory answer can be found there. However, when we encounter this dumbfounded state, too often we think there is nothing to be found, so we abandon the question. Because we identify with things, we move on to other things. Because we identify with the mind, we redirect our efforts so we can once again engage in our mental gymnastics.

How then are we to proceed if we cannot rely on even sophisticated, scientific, philosophical, or spiritual answers that are formulated through mental activity? When we exhaust the course of our thoughts and come to a dead end of the mind, what then? If we turn around and simply go another direction, if we redirect our attention onto other things, we will abandon all the progress made to get this far. Instead, what if, in the face of this great non-answer, we stay with the question?

In this unknowing state, a kind of spaciousness may open up, a vast emptiness. Now, undisturbed by thoughts, what are you aware of? Even here, at the very edge of the mind, the imagined "I" cannot be found. When you look, it vanishes. And here in this space, in this profound unknowing, it is possible through grace to let go of it forever.

Direct Investigation

Wherever you direct your inquiry, one way to begin is through direct investigation. Don't trust anything you have read or anything anybody has told you to be the case. Get your proverbial hands dirty and examine your own thoughts, emotions, sensations, and perceptions directly within your awareness. Try to see if you can determine anything through this examination.

Imagine yourself to be a kind of detective or scientist, only set the bar for proof or disproof higher than any criminal investigation or scientific study. In those endeavors, one seeks evidence in order to adopt a workable theory, model, or explanation of one's observations. But in the type of investigation I'm suggesting, workable is not good enough. In this investigation, we are seeking the absolute truth itself.

Relatively speaking, given sufficient observations and evidence, we might prove beyond a reasonable doubt that Joe Blow deliberately planned and carried out the theft of the famous Watts Diamond. But can we be certain the past is even the past? Can we be certain, now that it is missing, that the Watts Diamond ever existed? Can we be certain that Joe Blow is actually an individual capable of doing anything of his own free will?

The purpose of such an investigation is not to narrow down the possibilities, but to open the possibilities by examining and observing our most fundamental assumptions and faculties. At least initially, the goal is not to decrease the level of uncertainty, but instead to increase it, by calling everything into question.

It's difficult to give specific instruction here, since the avenues of inquiry are so vast. Take whatever is in front of you now, wherever you are, whatever you are doing. Look at an object, for instance, any object. What is it aside from an image, a form in the visual field? Perhaps if you lean in and smell it you may become aware of an aroma. Was the aroma there before you were aware of it? Is there any way to know if it was? Can you be sure that the object is solid before you pick it up? Now that you've picked it up, look at the place it was a moment ago. Can you be certain that it was there? What happened to that moment a moment ago?

What's happening that makes you think what you think about all these things? What memories and thoughts and sensations arise? Look inward and try to find where they are coming from. Can you find their source? Is it even possible not to be thinking these thoughts in this moment? Is it possible not to be doing exactly what you are doing right now, whatever it is?

Examine your thoughts to make sure you are not making any assumptions. Check things out. Test everything through your experience — time, sleep, memory, emotions, consciousness, identity, and so on. See if you can discover what's really happening.

This is the kind of investigation I'm talking about. If you take your assumptions for granted, these questions may seem silly, and if you're not really interested in the truth you may shy away from this type of investigation all together. But if you assume nothing … well then … all bets are off.

FROM WHERE DOES THIS FEELING ARISE?

There is a particular feeling we have of being in a body, possessing a mind, inhabiting a world, struggling to survive, as we move through time between birth and death. We have given this feeling the name *life*, and so we say, "I am alive. I am here. I am this body. I am this mind."

Whatever it is, search for this feeling or combination of feelings that makes you think you are alive in this body, that you are here in this world. Try to identify what it is. When you think you have identified it, ask yourself: *Is it always present? Is it there when I am dreaming, or when I am in the deepest sleep?* If it isn't, and you do not deny your existence in these other states, then perhaps that particular feeling is not what you really are. Perhaps it is just a feeling, and the thoughts that accompany it are just thoughts.

Many, many feelings may arise — many sights, many sounds, many sensations, many emotions, many thoughts — all entangled with each other. But they all come and go, arise and subside. Not a single one of them, nor any combination of them, can be held on to or sustained. Whatever feeling or experience you identify as the conditions for your existence, they cannot be sustained, even from day to day, hour to hour, moment to moment.

So here is a deeper question: What is always present … and what is the feeling of that?

When faced with this question, often we do not know where to begin. That is precisely *because* it is always present. We cannot stand outside of it and recognize it through contrast. We cannot see it as other than our true Self, and we cannot see our true Self because we are looking for something *other* while thinking we are something we are not.

How, then, to proceed?

Stop seeking something other than what you are already. Instead, find out what you are. Stop seeking to identify yourself through any limitation. Instead, find out whether any limitation exists.

Whatever feeling arises, ask yourself: *From where does this feeling arise? Whose feeling is it? What is its source?*

A Peculiar Emptiness

If you pursue your inquiry long enough, with sufficient attention and determination, you may begin to detect a peculiar emptiness around the edges of the mind. When you catch a glimpse of this emptiness, you may think there's not anything there, as if to pursue that further would be a fruitless venture with regard to your inquiry. All your life you've been conditioned to ignore such emptiness, but if you are seeking the truth, this *not-anything* is actually what you are looking for.

When determination to find an answer meets an impossible question, the mind goes into a kind of cognitive dissonance. It may bounce from one possibility to another, but find no purchase. If sustained, there is no place for it to settle, nothing for it to grasp. In the space between and behind all possibilities is this peculiar emptiness.

What is it?

Well ... it doesn't seem to be anything at all. That's the peculiar thing about it. It's a kind of no-thing, about which nothing can be said. But it's always there.

When first discovered, a person may find this disturbing. A person is identified with the ego, and discovery of this emptiness suggests that behind the ego is also this emptiness. This threatens the existence of the ego as a real and separate being, and so our instinct is to cover it up or to ignore it and walk away.

In a nutshell, that is the difficulty of spiritual inquiry. Instead of being offered more and more answers — a kind of accumulation of egoic understanding — a person is offered less and less. In fact, if you succeed, you may get rid of *you* all together, and instead there will just be this emptiness. Let's be honest, to the ego, it doesn't seem like a very good selling point.

To the ego, however, the Reality is unimaginable, because the ego depends on separation for its existence. This emptiness is also the complete fullness of being. And the ultimate goal of spiritual inquiry is the spontaneous realization of this being as consciousness itself, as the truth, as the source of everything, as the Self, as the all-pervading God, as the one and only indivisible Reality.

And all this is to say, if you ever feel like your inquiry isn't getting you anywhere, that you are no closer to the answers you seek than you were at the beginning, that in fact you know less than you ever did, keep going. Never cease longing for the truth.

4

EXISTENTIAL DREAD

What we long for is what we are most afraid to find out.

IN THE BACK OF THE MIND

Way in the back of the mind, we know there is something we cannot escape, but we don't really know what it is. We have done our best to cover it up, to hide from it, to ignore it, or to think we have it all figured out, but it's always there. We imagine it in various ways, sometimes trying to understand what it is without looking right at it, sometimes just trying to get away from it. We may imagine it as God. We may imagine it as death. We may imagine it as chaos, insanity, or the devil himself. We may imagine it as emptiness, meaninglessness, guilt, or despair. But however we imagine it, we are only imagining.

Just as an experiment, let's try to actually see what's in the back of the mind.

Try for a moment to look at the back of your head. But don't look into a mirror. I don't mean the outside of your head, but the inside. Look through the middle of it. Quite literally, try to picture what is behind the eyes. Don't roll your eyes back into your sockets, though. That's not what I mean. And I don't mean for you to imagine or visualize your optic nerve or your brain in some way, or anything else you think you know about. Let your eyes relax and just look for a moment at what's going on in the visual field. There's this image in front … and now try to picture what is in back. What color is it? What shape? What limits does it have?

The back of your head is actually like this something way in the back of your mind. You can never really see it … because it's you. But also, it may seem like there's nothing there. Just focusing on the visual field, suddenly it can seem as if you have no head at all! Or, it may suddenly occur to you that the back of your head is actually just the flip side of the image you are seeing. And this, as you might imagine, could all be very disturbing. Where could all your thoughts be knocking around if you do not have a head? And what exactly is it that you're looking at?

Luckily, as we know, we all have heads. Right? Just feel with your hand or look in the mirror and set yourself at ease. And of course, your brain is inside. It's been verified that brains are inside heads countless times. And that's where you must be knocking about in. Whew!

And yet … there's still that something way in the back of the mind. You cannot quite see it, nor can you entirely forget about it, either.

There still seems to be something we've overlooked, something we've left out of the picture. There still seems to be some inescapable fact that we're ignoring. We've kept it hidden, even from ourselves, but it's always threatening to come to light. What could it be?

Could it be the soul? The spirit? Whatever it is, it seems to go right to the heart of our existence. It seems to touch upon the very source of our being? It seems to prompt the very questions we've been asking. Who or what are you?

Could it be whatever God we believe in … whatever heaven we imagine, whatever hell we fear?

Could it be a sneaking suspicion that everything is meaningless … a pointless cascade of suffering and despair?

Could it just be death, that inescapable end that we cannot grasp … a nothing into which our eyes cannot gaze?

Whatever we do, however we imagine it, we cannot seem to look directly at this something in the back of the mind. We may long to know what it is. We may imagine it is something grim and just want to know. We may imagine it is something good, and want to attain it. But if a moment arises when we could *really* look directly at it, we may be overcome with fear. If we happen to catch a glimpse of it, we may be filled with mortal terror. Faced with it, we may feel flooded with an existential dread that permeates every corner of the mind.

The Specter of Death

Insert *Hamlet* soliloquy here, allow sufficient time to ponder the end of things … and now let's talk a little about death. Few are eager to have the conversation. Fewer still are eager to cross the threshold. For the most part, the attitude is to put death off — put off thinking about it, put off talking about it, and by all means put off the thing itself. For so many people, regardless of belief or non-belief in any sort of afterlife, this is the big existential crux. So let's go into it a bit.

Before we go on, I should say that I am not here to give to you any metaphysical, spiritual, or other-worldly model for or story about what's going to happen to you after you die. If you're worried about that, you've already got a story. Anything I may say is by way of understanding how you may see things now, and maybe of seeing things differently. As always, you should endeavor to conduct your own inquiry. What are you really … and what dies? And, of course, what is death if not just the end of something?

At some point we become identified with a body and mind and a sense of its continuity through life, from an imagined birth to an imagined death. Although we may not remember our birth or being an infant, we still in some way think, *That was me.* Even the memories we have are only present memories. That is, the past is not actually present, and yet we still think, *That was me.* And although the death we anticipate in the future is never what is happening now, we still in some way think, *I will undergo that.*

On the other hand, when we examine closely what's really happening at any moment, we may see on some level that if we are here now, whatever is happening, that's all there is. That's everything!

And yet, we have seen death. The body stops working, the activity of the mind disappears, and the familiar patterns of a person's life no longer arise. Certainly the decay of the body and cessation of mind can be observed in others. Naturally, if we believe ourselves to be a body and a mind, then death is the end of us, and so is the focus of so much fear and dread.

As long as we are identified with a body and a mind, the specter of death is ever present. For we know intuitively that what is born will die, what arises will subside, what appears will disappear, what comes into existence will fall out of existence. That is the way of things, the way of bodies, the way of minds, the way of egos, the way of worlds. As we continue in our spiritual journey, we are drawn near to the end of all things, and for this reason a sudden fear of death may arise at any moment.

To overcome this death and the dread that it engenders, one cannot seek always to guard against it, to fight it, or to run away from it. I don't mean to say one should seek their own death, but when fear of death, the imagined death, or even the actual death arises, one should go right into it and find out what it really is.

When I tell you that there is no death, I do not mean that the body will not decay, that the activity of the mind will not dissipate. I mean that death is only an idea about the passing of illusions. For the body is like a dream which arises in the morning and disappears at night. And the mind is like a shape in the clouds, which is there one moment, gone the next. All of this is the play of illusion. Birth and death are no different.

When body and mind and everything else are no longer present, what has been lost, and what remains? *That* is the question.

Insanity & Annihilation

People worry not only about the dissolution of the body, but also of the mind whilst the body yet lives. We may fear the depths of depression, anxiety, and other neurosis. We may fear dementia or senility, or any other condition that would destroy or degrade the mind-body state that we think we are. Of course, we should be prudent in the presence of any mental illness or medical condition. But on a deeper level, what we really fear is a loss of control over our view of ourselves and the world.

As the spiritual journey continues, this fear may intensify. If the view of no-view comes into view, if one glimpses the state of no-state, it's possible that we may worry less about death and more about insanity or self-annihilation, through the dissolution of the mind. In this case, while we may not fear the imminent demise of the body, we may fear that to go further would lead into madness. We cannot imagine a state of no-state, and so we imagine only self-annihilation, and we cannot have that.

To be clear, this too is a function of identification with the mind and body. The ego is an imagined self, composed of the repetition and coordination of various thoughts, emotions, and sensations. It involves belief in various concepts, interpretations, and ideas resulting from mind and body identification. When the ego forms, we mistakenly believe it to be the substance of who and what we are. But it is only the coordination of mind-body elements that creates the illusion of a separate individual who is real and permanent within some limitation of time and space.

If we believe that this is what we are, an individual and separate mind and body, existing in an objectified, external world, and that these and their relationships to each other constitutes reality, then what is one to think when these ideas, divisions, and relationships begin to break down? What are we likely to feel if these things suddenly become transparent, without boundaries, and without limits? If we still cling to our beliefs — and our idea of ourselves — we are likely to think we are losing our minds.

Actually, we may have merely begun to see through our own conceptualized version of reality. What may have happened is that, perhaps for a moment, we saw clearly. But this primordial clarity is so different from the way things are seen through the ego that it's quickly labeled an anomaly, hallucination, trick of the mind, or losing one's mind. We may flee back to the familiar way of seeing things, to experiencing an objectified world through an individual and separate ego-self.

Note, however, that all thoughts, all ideas of who we are and what reality is, are impermanent. Any conceptualization of our existence can be shattered, dissolved, or transcended. Reality itself is impossible to break. Consider carefully which is madness and which is clarity.

Fear of Enlightenment

On the path to enlightenment, when we draw near to the truth, we may be overcome with a sense of inexplicable fear. Although this fear can be attributed to the fear of death, fear of losing one's mind, or simply the fear of losing the individual ego-self and all our treasured things, beliefs, and views, it can also be understood as a fear of enlightenment itself.

For one thing, we may be afraid of being left with nothing. The search itself has its own delights, and the excitement of the quest carries its own fascination. In this way, we are like children, who do not want the game to end, even if we are tired and irritable. We want the fun of the play to go on. The thought of having no questions left, nothing to search for, no drama to anticipate, no winning or losing, and no future happiness to look forward to may not sound very appealing to the average person. The thought of primordial wisdom may actually sound scary.

In all traditions that speak of God, the presence of God can be terrifying. How much more terrifying to lose oneself in that unbound, infinite, all-encompassing awareness? The secret, of course, is we are *that* already, but do not realize it. And while this realization is something we long for, once the fire of inquiry has been kindled, it is also the very thing that the ego-self fears most. For in the presence of divine awareness, we must not just become nothing, but realize we have never been anything but that, without beginning and without end. The entirety of our imagined life is like a brief and ephemeral wave on the surface of a vast ocean, from which we have never been apart.

The fear may arise not only in relation to the ego's death, but also with the intuition that we were never really born and so cannot really die. The fear may arise not just in recognizing that we may lose our mind, but with the intuition that we have no mind to lose. These intuitions, these possibilities, truly wondrous when fully realized, are impossible to imagine beforehand. So while enlightenment may be longed for, the idea of it may still inspire some fear.

We may think: *What can all that mean? What will that be like?* But such questions are formed in delusion, in the context of the very dualities and divisions that awakening would erase. Perhaps it will put this fear into perspective to say that the fear is just a fear of thoughts, a fear of ideas. What's happening is already happening. There is nothing to gain or lose. Perhaps it will be more productive to ask: To whom is the fear? To whom will be the enlightenment? Find that out, and all fears will be assuaged.

RESISTANCE TO TRUTH

If the truth is ultimately liberation, why is there such resistance to it? If the ego-self is unreal, why does it hold such sway over our lives? If there is nothing to fear, why are we so afraid? If existence is the unending joy of pure awareness, why so much dread?

These are excellent questions. They are difficult ones to answer because they go right to the source of everything and our confusion about it.

There is no doubt that this resistance, this dread, and this suffering seems to exist for us. But can it be understood or eradicated through an explanation or an examination of the situation?

Not exactly. Grasping the situation or explaining it is not enough, or rather is too much, for any grasping or explaining is actually a part of the resistance in question.

Intricate and subtle philosophies can be of great use in pointing the way toward the truth, as well as in exhausting the faculties of the ordinary mind. But the problem is not one of complexity. In fact, complexity implies a multitude of parts, concepts, relationships, and interactions. And even in the realm of ideas, this is the wrong idea. Ultimately, it is more a problem of profound simplicity, of a oneness so radical that the ordinary mind cannot possibly grasp it.

We could blame ignorance, as if it were something we were subjected to against our will, but find out to whom this ignorance exists and suddenly there is no ignorance at all. We could blame maya or the power of illusion, but find out to whom these illusions appear and no illusions remain. This suggests that no outside force can be the cause of such resistance. It is our own doing. Perhaps we could blame the ego then, but we soon find the ego is just a manifestation of ignorance and illusion.

These are all metaphors by way of explanation. Focusing on any particular one, we miss that none can stand outside of everything. Even ignorance is arising within the absolute clarity of pure awareness. Our search must go deeper if we are to let go of our resistance, our fear, our dread, and realize our nature as this radical oneness.

Consider, then, that there may be nowhere to place the blame ... because in fact, there is nothing amiss.

PART II

THE SEARCH

5

FAR FROM HOME

Nobody said this would be easy ...

The Wandering Spirit

The seeker on the journey can be imagined as a kind of wandering spirit, far from home. Here and there the spirit goes, according to the circumstances it is born into and the situations it encounters.

In the beginning this spirit may not even be conscious of the profound nature of its journey. It may merely be seeking out pleasures according to its desires, grasping at whatever it believes will give it more pleasure, and trying to avoid the pain and suffering that comes its way. The spirit may do this for quite some time, until something disturbs its activity.

The spirit may notice, for example, that no matter what it experiences, attains, or acquires, it cannot find lasting peace or happiness, and the elusive root of its desires is never really satisfied.

The spirit may be deeply troubled by its suffering or the suffering of others.

The spirit may also catch a glimpse of something beyond mere pleasure and pain, or beyond what it thinks itself or the world to be. And these glimpses — experienced as altered states, mystical visions, spiritual dreams, spontaneous insights, and so on — suggest a reality exists beyond what it has conceptualized.

Once the spirit is disturbed, the quest takes on a whole new character. While still compelled to grasp at pleasures and cling to safety, the spirit is now also aware of a greater goal. Although it may not be able to articulate fully what it is, or it may mistake the goal for a more subtle pleasure or attainment, this goal is nothing other than awakening. With this greater goal in mind, the seeker may read books and scriptures, find a teacher, and engage in a wide array of spiritual practices. But because the spirit is still grasping, it becomes divided, at war with itself, and suffering may actually increase.

On our own journey as a wandering spirit, we may experience subtle frustrations and great torments. Nagging dissatisfaction, broken hearts, despair, confusion, fear, envy, rage, self-loathing, and so on, are all possible waypoints on the seeker's journey. Self-sabotage, alcoholism, drug use, abusive relationships, depression, anxiety, escapism, and so on, are all possible symptoms of our spiritual malaise.

In the midst of such trials, we may feel like there's no way out. But I want to assure you, that whatever you are experiencing, no matter how horrible or how long it has been going on, it is only temporary. Don't give up! If only we continue on our quest, there is a way forward and there is a way out. It may not all be as you imagine it, or even as you think you want it, but it is nothing less than perfection. Ultimately, this wandering spirit always finds its way home.

SPIRITUAL LITERATURE

There is a treasure to be found in the world's spiritual literature, from ancient times to the modern day, and from religious scriptures to popular books. That is not to say it's all gold and heavenly gems — some of it is misleading at best — but in the recorded words of true saints, sages, and mystics from all the world's spiritual traditions the real teaching shines through. Although these texts come from different cultures, were composed in different languages, and proclaim, describe, and explain the truth each according to their background, disposition, insight, and experience, there is remarkable consistency when it comes to the essentials.

Those brought up in an established religious tradition may have been taught a somewhat literal, dogmatic, and simplistic interpretation of the tradition's texts. We may not have been exposed to mystical teachings, nor encouraged to test what they say against our own experience. In the West at least, that has meant we often encounter mystics from other traditions first. Perhaps later we discover them in our own tradition, or see the mystics as offering insight into all the traditions.

Unfortunately, when encountering the ancient scriptures or even the writings of modern mystics and spiritual teachers, the insight and clarity I speak of may not be immediately apparent. In fact, these texts may be downright baffling to anybody really trying to figure them out. Sure, some of it might make sense, but they nevertheless speak of a knowledge we cannot seem to get, an experience we cannot seem to bring about, or a place we cannot seem to find.

Why is it so difficult? First, there is a language problem, and it's not just the matter of translation — although that no doubt adds to the difficulties. Unlike almost every other type of literature, spiritual literature ultimately aims at that which is beyond all words. So no matter how carefully constructed the texts are, and no matter how eloquently written, they cannot simply take the reader to where they are pointing. They can only point, and they can only do that using the language and metaphors available. The seeker must realize for themselves what is beyond all words.

But the difficulty goes even deeper than that. In reading these strange and baffling texts, we expect the words must at least point to some inexpressible mental formulation. We might think that while the referent of these texts may be impossible to *say,* surely it can be thought. If we could just figure out that thought … if we could just figure out the proper mind set, then we would get it. But this too is a mistake. For such texts point to that which is not only beyond all words, but beyond all thought.

This is why a serious exploration of spiritual literature can be so frustrating for the determined seeker. If you have ever experienced this frustration in your reading, don't despair. Keep reading! While we may feel confused, just reading such texts can have an imperceptible effect on us. Beyond our own understanding, they can push us — sometimes very gently and sometimes quite abruptly — toward awakening.

Spiritual Traps

When we talk about spiritual traps, we could just as easily speak of eddies and whirlpools in a freely-flowing stream. However, that itself can be a trap if we are still seeking. While effort is still needed on the journey, it is more useful to note them as traps one may fall into, so we can consider how best to get out of them.

Complacency and ambition are the two basic branches of all the spiritual traps. On the one hand, we may lack sufficient interest, aspiration, faith, or intention to put forth effort in practice. On the other hand, we may have plenty of interest and aspiration, even faith, but with the wrong intention — desiring to attain powers, experiences, fame, respect, acclaim, or so on.

Falling into the trap of complacency can manifest as settling in, and as an aversion to change, new insights, new challenges, or new directions for practice. Intellectually, we think we have things pretty well figured out, that we more-or-less know how things are.

This is complacency. Spiritually and emotionally, we can avoid doing the difficult work of practice by replacing it with easier commitments to superficial practices and appearances. This is also complacency. Complacency can result in deluded views, non-practice, and weak or ineffective practice. At the extreme this trap is exemplified by laziness, pride, cynicism, or callous indifference.

Falling into the trap of ambition can manifest as a desire for personal greatness or an obsession with obtaining spiritual powers, physical perfection, or extraordinary skills. Intellectually, we may become overly concerned with learning, understanding, and integrating conceptual models acquired through books and study. Emotionally we may feel envious of others and hope for high status and great acclaim. Spiritually, we may fixate on the attainment of special skills or powers, or on having blissful or otherwise extraordinary experiences. This is all ambition, and can result in deluded views, non-practice, and wrong or counterproductive practice. At the extreme this trap can be exemplified by narcissism, arrogance, despair, or greed.

That's all well and good, but this trap business is more subtle than it seems at first glance, and there is still the matter of how to escape from them. Therefore, it's important to mention that dosage matters. It helps to think of these traps as administering a kind of poison. Consider that even a good medicine can be a poison if taken at too high a dosage. And sometimes, what would normally be considered a poison, at just the right dosage, could be good medicine — or an antidote to another poison.

The antidote to complacency is nothing other than a proportional dose of ambition. And the antidote to ambition is nothing other than a proportional dose of complacency. At just the right dosage, one can neutralize the other.

How does it work?

Complacency and ambition only become poisonous when they are co-opted to sustain and fuel egoic desires. Complacency is a form of indifference, and freed from ego-identification, has its roots in equanimity. Ambition is a form of desire, and freed from ego-identification, has its roots in a will to the truth or a longing for God. So complacency and ambition have within them good medicine. The medicine must be administered selflessly and proportionally, but when it is, the patient gets well and can continue on their journey.

FINDING A TEACHER

The real spiritual teacher, the true guru, and so on, is nothing other than reality itself, nothing other than God, nothing other than the Self. They are all the same. In the service of grace, to aide you on your journey, the teacher will appear in a variety of forms. This great teacher can appear through books and lectures, traditions and religious services, through friends, loved ones, and complete strangers. The teacher can appear in the sun and moon and stars, in the wayward glance, in the meeting of eyes, in the briefest touch. The teacher can appear in dreams, at the brink of exhaustion, in the agony of pain, in the depths of grief, in resounding silence, and in the midst of sensual delight.

How wonderful that this great teacher can appear in everything and everyone! How wonderful that this guru of gurus is nothing other than the one Self, our own true nature!

While we are yet abroad, however, far from home and still on our journey, the challenge is in recognizing and cultivating a relationship with an appearance or appearances of this teacher. To some extent, this too is a matter of circumstances and personal tendencies. We cannot help but follow our inclinations and interests. But we *can* follow them with some diligence, and set our intentions on finding a suitable teacher for wherever we happen to be on our journey.

It is possible to find a teacher in a dream or in the form of an animal, a forest, even a rock. We have already established that the teacher can appear in many forms. Generally speaking, however, we often need a teacher in the form of a person.

To have a good, productive relationship with a teacher, we need to be open to learning, open to change, and open to letting go. We do not have to give up our critical thinking, but if we have no faith that the teacher has insight beyond our own, why take the person as a teacher? If we are only willing to look at what our mind has already encompassed, if we are only willing to go where we feel secure and comfortable, we are not open to learning, not open to change, and not open to letting go. To the extent that we set our intentions on being open, consciously or unconsciously, there is space for the teaching to enter.

The teacher needs to be a person who can point out mistakes in our practice, guide us out of spiritual traps, and administer antidotes to whatever poisons we have ingested. The teacher should be a person who can help us see things differently, challenge us to let go of our attachments, and shock us into dropping conditioned thoughts. We would do well to find a person with deep practice and keen knowledge in whatever practice or tradition we are interested in. Ultimately, we can hope for nothing more than to find an awakened teacher with skill in pointing students toward the truth.

Engaging in Practice

Whatever religious or spiritual tradition we happen to have a connection with or are inclined to participate in, to make progress we cannot just stand idly by like a fly on the wall. If we wish for transformation, we need to engage in the practices that present themselves in the context of our lives. We need to seek out teachers who can challenge our entrenched views and help us on the path. We need to move our bodies, engage our minds, and open our hearts.

Everything that is necessary is already at hand, but nevertheless it is helpful to recognize and engage in practice. Whether we follow a particular religion or have no religious beliefs and no formal spiritual practice, the need and the help is the same.

We should not expect miracles. We should not be dismayed if the practice does not immediately make us feel more spiritual or more capable of handling ourselves or the difficulties of our lives. The day-to-day practice may even feel quite mundane. We may feel like we are not doing very well. We may feel we are hopelessly bad at it. These are just feelings. Keep engaging in the work of spiritual practice, and the miracles will take care of themselves.

Remember that our practices are not a way of attaining knowledge, acquiring merit, or perfecting ourselves. They are a way of helping us to let go of whatever we need to let go of … and ultimately, to let go of everything. No practice can take us to the very end of our journey, so we should understand each practice as having built into its advanced stages a way of letting go of the practice itself. Don't be surprised if you discover disillusionment. Disillusionment and emptying are all a part of the greater practice that is the whole of our spiritual journey.

If we do not have a regular practice or feel inclined to try a new practice, we need to seek one out and commit to it, at least for a while. If we already have a practice or practices that we feel are helpful — be it attending a religious service, a weekly yoga class, or a daily meditation — we can commit to going deeper into it, to uncovering the hidden layers of practice within each practice, and to expanding our understanding of what it is we are doing. And we can set our intention to let go of the untrue, the unreal, and all our selfish and deluded desires.

The next two chapters will explore practices and particular routes in more detail. To find our way on this path, it is not enough to entertain spiritual thoughts, read a few books, or passively show up to a meeting, a lecture, or a service. We must put the teachings into practice. Only then can we see where they really lead.

6

QUIETING THE
MIND-BODY-WORLD

The true way is without effort,
and yet we can only approach through effort.

A MODEL FOR SPIRITUAL PRACTICE

If we examine our thoughts carefully, we will probably find that
we have a lot of ideas about what the mind and body are, how they
came to be, and how they are related to our ego or sense of self.
But if we go on to question our ideas deeply, we may discover that
instead of feeling like we know more and more about these things,
we feel as if we know less and less. We may come to see that our
thoughts and ideas about the mind, body, ego, and self are only
thoughts, only ideas, and we don't really know what these things
are, after all.

Ultimately, we may realize they are nothing at all. To get to that point, however, some kind of model may be useful in dealing with the mind and body.

Mind, body, and ego arise through a process of identification with accumulated patterns of thoughts, emotions, and sensations. The more dense the accumulations and the more interconnected the patterns, the more identified we become with them. Mind, body, and ego are the base of individual identity and all separation. This truth is not apparent, though, because we are already identified with them when they come into being. Thus arises dissatisfaction, suffering, and fear of death.

The ego-self and its entanglements — mind and body — are like a mask. None are the true Self. To realize the true Self, we must take off our mask. But already being identified with the mask, how can we take it off? The feeling we have is that we *are* this mask. How, then, can we remove it? And what could possibly be behind it? And so the search begins to find out what is really behind the mask of ourselves.

We can begin attempting to deconstruct the ego by first deconstructing the mind and body. Deconstruction may sound like a daunting or suicidal task, though. So perhaps it is more helpful to think of rendering the mask transparent. If we can clarify the substance of the mask enough, perhaps we can simply see through it. What lies beyond will naturally be revealed.

The search, then, might proceed through clarification of mind and body. In many traditions, the word *purification* is used. Whatever our model or choice of words — deconstruct, clarify, purify — there is still the practical matter of how to go about it.

Thousands of years of traditions have left us an abundance of good practices: meditation, prayer, yoga, ascetic disciplines, rituals, contemplation, vision quests, et cetera. Often, however, our practice lacks focus or proper intention because we have no model for understanding the underlying purpose. Many of the traditional models may not resonate with us, and many modern models leave out the actual goal.

Here I will offer a very simple model, as a kind of signpost should anyone choose to follow it. Mind and body are composed of various forms of tension. These are the accumulations and patterns of thoughts, emotions, and sensations. The overall pattern of these tensions is what it feels like to be you, and identification with it results in the ego.

Physical tension can be thought of as tightness within and between the muscles, tendons, bones, connective tissues, nerves, blood vessels, lymph channels, and all the various parts of the body. Psychological tension can be thought of as conflict that arises within and between thoughts and emotions. Such conflicts manifest as fear, anger, anxiety, self-pity, indecision, confusion, and despair, as well as desire, lust, greed, self-importance, and so on. Tensions can also exist between mind and body, and between mind, body, ego, and other minds, bodies, egos, and objects.

With this model, we can understand all the various spiritual practices as ways of locating, quieting, and letting go of various tensions. Release of tension allows for a kind of neutral or clarified state. Of course, there is always the opportunity to instantly see through it all and realize what is beyond everything. Grace is ever-present, and one cannot move closer to the absolute. But the clarification of these tensions provides opportunities for insight. After realization, the ego dissolves, and whatever tensions appear thereafter are rendered transparent.

The spiritual journey, then, can progress through practices aiming at recognizing, understanding, and releasing tension, be it physical, intellectual, or emotional. That much can be pursued as a spiritual path and as creating opportunities for insight. Realization of the true Self, however, ultimately remains a matter of grace.

CLARIFYING THE MIND

Meditation has long been associated with the spiritual path, and for good reason. It is a powerful tool for quieting the mind and examining our actual experience. Almost everyone who has ventured down a spiritual path has encountered meditation in some form, even if they don't call it that. There are many types of meditation practices, and instruction varies greatly. But let us ask: What are the fundamental methods? What are the essential practices? Let us see if we can come to a broader understanding of meditation, and perhaps more importantly find some direction for practice.

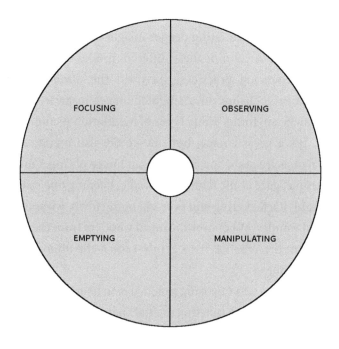

I have here divided various types of meditation into four basic modes of practice: Focusing, Observing, Manipulating, and Emptying. In the course of actual practice, there is certainly crossover, but there is also a sequence. Strictly speaking, there is no hierarchy of practices, and while the routes vary, all practices spiral toward the one true Self. However, observation will be difficult without a steady mind developed through focusing. Manipulation will be fruitless without the inquiring attitude cultivated through observation. Emptying may yield no insight without some knowledge of what is being emptied out. Focusing will be impossible without the ability to empty out distracting thoughts. So it is more of a circle or spiral than a line, with each mode of practice facilitating deeper insight into the others. With that in mind let's examine these different modes of practice.

With Focusing practices, we train the attention toward steadiness by focusing on a singular object in awareness. This object can be anything. Many types of meditation recommend the breath. It's a great choice, but one could also meditate on an external object, a mantra, a prayer, or an image of God. One could, for example, gaze at the flame of a candle, keeping one's attention on its light, it's flickering and ever-changing form, without letting the mind wander. Whenever the mind wanders from the object of meditation, the practice is to gently return the attention to the meditation object.

The purpose of a Focusing practice is to be mindful of what is happening and to start quieting mental chatter. When we first start such a practice, we may notice just how wildly our attention wanders and how many distracting thoughts, emotions, and sensations arise when we attempt to tame it. Each phenomenon represents a kind of tension. Some create desire, others aversion, others indifference. If we follow them, they will lead to more thoughts, more emotions, and more sensations, perpetuating a cycle of wandering mental activity, and reinforcing whatever conditioned patterns of tension exist within the mind. Just by noting what these distractions are, and not following them — by instead returning the attention to the singular object of meditation — we start to break the cycles of conditioning, and the mind begins to quiet down.

This is already a notable achievement, if we can speak in those terms. And Focusing practices are incredibly useful. For example, when anxiety or troubling thoughts assail you, calm yourself by turning your attention to an object of meditation. If followed, this practice can grant deep insight. There are many more meditation practices, however, and it is useful to explore them all.

With Observing practices, we inquire into the nature of objects and our distractions by observing various phenomena. One example is the observation of thoughts, watching how they appear and disappear in the clear field of consciousness. This type of observation can be applied to anything. Whether the phenomena seems to be inside or outside is irrelevant, since all phenomena are actually appearing in same field of consciousness. So in this way, we can observe thoughts, emotions, sensations, the body, or any object that appears in our awareness. Cultivating a disposition of curiosity, trace all phenomena to their origin and ultimate end. From where do they arise? To where do they go?

With Manipulating practices, we can experiment with manipulating mental forms. Many practices fall into this category. We could try visualizing deities or mandalas. We could try creating and transforming geometric shapes in the darkness behind closed eyes. We could stare at a candle flame and then try sustaining its image after closing the eyes. We could try forming imaginary landscapes, complete with sounds and smells, tastes and textures. We could also try inducing out-of-body experiences, entering lucid dreams, or various altered mind states.

Such practices can provide powerful insight, but they can also be a rabbit hole of sensational abilities and experiences. If we merely chase after such experiences for our own enjoyment or selfish desires, with no regard for the ultimate goal of such practice, without honest inquiry into the truth, we are missing the point, and could risk hampering rather than aiding our spiritual progress. A teacher could be very helpful here. As with observations, one should trace the malleability of all mental forms back to their origin. In short, who is the creator and manipulator of all such forms?

Finally, with Emptying practices, we seek directly to give up all active focusing, observing, and manipulating. But we give up focusing by giving up the focuser. We give up observing by giving up the observer. And we give up manipulating by giving up the manipulator. The emptying practice is one of not doing anything ... and not *not* doing anything. Whatever arises, let it be as it is, without seeking to hold it or get rid of it. We may begin by attempting to let go of whatever arises and surrender to the flow of phenomena. But this letting go is just not grasping, and this surrender is just not resisting. So even though this emptying is just not doing, we give up this doing by giving up the doer. Still, this practice is just emptying. That's all it is.

There are so many kinds of meditation that whatever we do or don't do in our meditation may qualify as practice, especially if the intention is toward surrendering the ego and realization of the truth. As we quiet the mind more and more, letting go of attachment to its various activities, it is possible to see the mind itself, in its entirety, as an object within awareness, and to let go of that as well. In this way, identification with the mind comes to an end.

Clarifying the Body

Many traditions combine the meditative practices with practices designed to understand, develop, and clarify the body. Various types of massage and healing arts, as well as dance, yoga, martial arts, and even activities like free diving or mountain climbing, at their highest levels, necessarily involve the practitioner with an inquiry into the nature of the body and self. If one persists in such a practice, it may progress beyond a struggle to attain higher levels of skill, and into a struggle to understand oneself completely. This is not surprising, since mind and body are not separate, and the ego is identified with both. The deep study of the body, like the deep study of the mind, will eventually run into the ego and all its entanglements.

The history of our life, with all its victories and traumas, are written in the tissues of the body. The patterns of tension that exist within the mind are reflected in the patterns of tension that exist within the body. Therefore, practices that clarify physical tension help to clarify mental tension, and vice versa. Remember that while the removal of some tensions and the restructuring of the overall tension pattern may be an important step, simply removing all tension is not the goal, nor is the creation of a perfect tension pattern. The goal is clarification, to see and understand the process through which we identify with the present pattern, and thereby break the cycle of identification.

To this end, body-centered practices can be divided into the same four basic modes as meditation: Focusing, Observing,

Manipulating, and Emptying. In this way, while the details of practice may differ, working on the body is no different than working on the mind. The intermediary goal may be a healthy body and a healthy mind, but the ultimate goal is clarification, to understand yourself, and thereby render body and mind transparent.

Strictly speaking, I want to be clear that meditation itself could be regarded as a very streamlined body practice, and all body practices involve meditative aspects, especially at higher levels. Practically speaking, however, body-centered practices are even more diverse than meditative practices, and any given practice is likely to contain multiple modes within it, so it is difficult to give specific examples without unduly emphasizing a particular practice or mode over another. But with that in mind, let's examine how the different modes appear in body-centered practices.

When it comes to body-centered practice, Focusing practices train the body toward steadiness within a particular form. In the larger context, this could just mean practicing regularly or mastering a set of postures, movements, or actions. While practicing, however, it means keeping one's attention on the training. This is just like meditation, with the training itself as the object of meditation. One should note any distractions and bring the attention back to the practice at hand. With training, the body begins to develop a base level of competence in the practice.

Observing practices go deeper into the body to explore in detail what is actually happening in the context of movement, stillness, exertion, and dynamic action. We can directly observe, in greater and greater detail, the various systems of the body and how they function, examining the breath, pulse and circulation, digestion, nervous system, muscular system, et cetera. Observe the static and dynamic tensions that exist within the body and the overall pattern they create. Turn awareness on the body itself, with ever greater sensitivity, and create an internal map of what is going on and how everything is happening.

Manipulating practices aim at changing tension levels and patterns in the body. This is the level at which various massage, health, and healing practices operate. By manipulating the physical and subtle structures of the body, overall tension levels can be lowered, and unhealthy patterns can be removed or restructured. Changes can also be made through exercises, diet, sleep, breath control, movement and relaxation, et cetera. Just as in meditation, there are various pitfalls in this mode of practice. Here too, one can become a chaser of experiences or become obsessed with developing certain powers, achieving perfection, or attaining ever-greater levels of performance or control. At a certain point, manipulation alone is a mistake — literally a dead end — that impedes progress rather than facilitates it. Manipulation should be balanced by emptying.

Emptying practices, with regard to the body, are less a matter of doing anything, and more a matter of letting things do themselves, or of simply letting go. Allow the body to carry on as it would, without interfering in any way, without judgment or recursive thoughts, and without attempting to focus, control, or even observe. The Emptying practice is one of letting go of the body, of ceasing to identify with its functions and actions. This represents a kind of *getting out of your own way.*

Remember, this is only a model. All the modes can be present in any single practice, manifesting according to instruction, intention, level, and circumstances. With regard to the spiritual journey, although complete emptying represents a final stage, the progression of practice should be seen as more of a spiral than a line, with some experience in each mode facilitating deeper insights into the other modes. In this way all the modes contribute from beginning to end — when the body itself, like the mind, may dissolve into consciousness.

CLARIFYING THE SOUL

If mind-body practices represent one approach to the spiritual quest, devotional and religious practices represent another, equally valid and complementary approach. While mind-body practices spiral inward toward the locus of self-identification, devotional practices spiral outward toward the *other*. The religious practitioner or devotee reaches outward, seeking the ultimate other, in the form of a guru, metaphysical concept, or God. Although the approach to practice is different, the end is the same. Realization of the true Self is none other than the realization of God, and vice versa.

With this in mind, we can examine devotional practices through the same modes as mind-body practices: Focusing, Observing, Manipulating, and Emptying. While the objects and direction of practice seem different, in truth there are no objects nor any direction, so all manifestations of spiritual practice ultimately have the same aim — although the practitioners may not know it, and the instructions and explanations for practice may not state it.

In devotional practices — following a religion, for example — Focusing practices are a matter of remembering God or whatever the ultimate conception may be. Regular practice, be it performing rituals or participating in ceremonies, songs, or prayers, trains the attention toward steadiness within the tradition and a particular conception of the divine. Through repeated remembrance, we are brought to contemplation.

The Observing practices are the methods of contemplation. Around us we observe the whole world and all its diversity in relation to our conception of God. We observe the good and the evil, the high and the low, the light and the dark, the familiar and the unfamiliar. And we wonder what, among all these things, is not under God. We begin to observe the world in such a way that our conceptions of the divine are continuously challenged.

The Manipulating practices involve changing our conception of God. We begin to expand our conception of God and God's grace, until it envelopes everything. We strive to see God's grace in all things. And through the course of these changes, we may take divinely-inspired action in the world, for such practices include loving kindness, charity, selfless acts, service, penance, pilgrimage, and so on. Through these, we attempt to live out our understanding of God in the world. Like all the Manipulating practices, the danger here is of perversion, of seeking out experiences solely for self-gratification, and of becoming stuck in action alone.

Ultimately, if our conception of God is to encompass everything, it must also encompass the individual self, and hence the focuser, the observer, and the manipulator. And so there is no place for the ego-self to remain apart. There is nothing we can do. Everything is as God wills it, and everything is done through God's omnipotence. Practices and prayers that acknowledge our helplessness, and that surrender the soul to God, letting go of the ego and of all claims to the individual self, the body, the mind, and the state of the world — these are the Emptying practices of devotion.

In the end, the supreme other, that in the beginning seems so different, so otherworldly, is recognized as not other, but as one's true Self. For there is none other than God. There is nothing but that. There never has been, nor will there ever be anything but that. For the Lord is One, eternal and without limitation.

TACKLING IMPOSSIBLE PROBLEMS

In the Zen tradition, koans may be used to point out mental tension and provide opportunities for clarification. The koan is a kind of riddle that is unsolvable by conventional thinking. It's a kind of impossible problem. The student is expected to meditate vigorously upon a koan and produce a solution. However, no constructed answer will do. The master will see through it immediately. When all the answers a student tries to come up with fail, the student really becomes stuck. An acceptable answer is only possible through a kind of spontaneous release or letting go, and can only come through clarification.

By working on the koan, one may go through all the different modes of practice: Focusing, Observing, Manipulating, and Emptying.

Unfortunately or fortunately as the case may be, not all of us have a Zen master to assign us riddles, press us into meditation, and judge our solutions for clarity. However, that shouldn't stop anybody on their spiritual quest. There are plenty of impossible problems in life's everyday situations. Even in Zen, a koan could be said to be more than just a riddle. For the Zen students, all of Zen and their involvement with it is the real koan. The riddle is just a manifestation of that.

The whole situation we find ourselves in — existence — is a kind of impossible problem. And in this way, all of life is a kind of Zen koan. You have already been assigned it. Perhaps you are already meditating upon it. All of life's situations, whatever is before you now, contains the essence of this great koan. And although you may not know it, you are your own master. You'll see, if you haven't already, that no constructed answer will satisfy you.

Go ahead, try to figure out what's really happening. Try to construct an answer to the riddle of the universe. Try to devise a solution to the problems in your life. Try to find lasting happiness or perfect satisfaction. Every day, we are confronted with the subtle mysteries of existence, with the demands of desire, action, and decision making. Moment to moment, we press ourselves into the meditation of everyday life, expecting to produce a solution.

You sit down to dinner, but cannot choose between the fish or the pasta. That's it! That is a koan. You find yourself in an untenable job, but you have to eat and pay the rent. That is a koan. You're tired of putting on your clothes and brushing your teeth, and yet day after day you have to do it. That is a koan. One day you start to think you made a mistake getting into your current relationship. That is a koan. You are diagnosed with a terminal illness and given six months to live. That is a koan.

Impossible problems take a multitude of forms, some subtle, some obvious. The subtle ones are easily ignored, and allow us to go on with our lives in the ignorance that arises from ignoring them. The obvious ones are more difficult to ignore, and press us forward on our spiritual journey, providing opportunities for greater clarification. Occasionally a problem comes along that is so impossible in the context of our life circumstances, and so intractable with regard to any solution, that we become well and truly stuck. Therein lies the possibility for totally letting go, for complete and spontaneous release, for the touch of grace ... and for enlightenment.

From the mundane to the profound, the situations of your life are continuously creating koans. You are a natural Zen master! You have an incredible intuitive knack for generating all these brilliant koans. All that's left is for you to solve the greatest koan of all — yourself.

7

PATHS TO TRUTH

Everything is a spiritual practice.

DIVERSITY IN SPIRITUAL PRACTICE

Before we begin the journey, we may think of spiritual practice as something for other people, as something that maybe isn't suited to our personality or our interests. We may think it requires certain beliefs or is only for the religious-minded person. We may think that a practical, logical, or scientific temperament precludes our involvement with spiritual practice. However, such preconceptions severely limit our idea of what the spiritual journey is, its relevance to our lives, and the diversity of practice.

If you have ever tried to obtain happiness or wished it upon others, if you have ever sought relief from suffering or recognized the suffering of others, you are already on the spiritual journey. You may not know it, but you have already set out upon the path.

Many aspects of what you are doing may be informed by this path — may already be a kind of unconscious spiritual practice.

Even when we consciously begin the journey, we may think of spiritual practice as a separate, compartmentalized part of our lives. The casual followers of various religions often regard their spiritual practices this way. We may think it all has to do with attending services, prayer, meditation, charity, and so on. The compartment may be larger or smaller according to the individual, but however we categorize our spirituality, we are still limiting our idea of the spiritual journey.

As the journey progresses, we may view more and more of our activity as a part of our spiritual practice. But as long as we remain deluded in some way, as long as we remain separate individuals, we will continue to have some level of compartmentalization. For we will, at the least, always view the objects of our practice as separate from ourselves.

In awakening, all separations are revealed as illusory. We have always been on the path. Not for a single moment have we ever strayed from it. Everything that has happened — every breath, every thought, every action, every effort — has been involved in this one great spiritual path.

Grace has always been present, and the spiritual journey *is* our lives, exactly as they are. So the possibilities and opportunities for spiritual practice are infinite. At any moment, we can focus our awareness on what is happening. Within every activity, we can set our intention toward awakening, toward the disillusionment of all our deluded concepts and selfish ideas. With every breath, we can turn toward God.

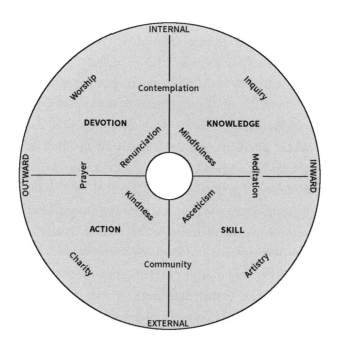

Mandala of Paths

According to circumstance and temperament, each will find their own path to the truth. Through an examination of the various spiritual traditions and practices, we can discern four main pathways, four approaches to the truth: Knowledge, Devotion, Action, and Skill. These paths can be mapped onto a mandala according to each path's focus and direction. Knowledge and Devotion have an internal focus, while Action and Skill have an external focus. Of the two internal paths, Knowledge is directed inward and Devotion is directed outward. Of the two external paths, Action is directed outward and Skill is directed inward.

I'm not entirely reinventing the wheel here. These categories basically exist already in the philosophical underpinnings of yoga. In the Indian tradition, three primary pathways are given. *Jnana* is a path of knowledge. *Bhakti* is a path of devotion. *Karma* is a path of action. To fill in our map we need only a path of skill. *Kriya* might fit. I am not a Sanskrit scholar, but the word *kriya* appears to mean "doing," "performing," "movement," or "action." Like *karma,* it comes from the root *kri* meaning "to do." Perhaps we could use both words to indicate the two external paths, with *Karma* directed outward and *Kriya* directed inward.

If you don't care for any of these names, we can also speak of Logic (knowledge), Faith (devotion), Works (action), and Art (skill). The categories can even be mapped onto the tarot's minor arcana, if you like that sort of thing. Swords are the path of knowledge, being associated with the intellect. Cups are the path of devotion, being associated with the emotions. Coins are the path of action, being associated with practical matters. And Wands are the path of skill, being associated with creativity. You get the idea. These are broad categories that appear in multiple traditions. So don't get too caught up in the names.

Before we go on, it's important to mention that this is just a conceptual map. As such, it can be an aid on the spiritual journey, but it is not the journey itself. If you find it helpful, great. If not, that's okay too. This map is designed to help you see that the path is wide and diverse. With the right intention, whatever you are doing already, and whatever you feel inclined to take up along the way, will surely fit into it.

Finally, I should say that while we're looking at four pathways here, in actuality there is only *the* path. A person is not meant to follow one of these four particular pathways, to the exclusion of the others, but rather to seek and find the truth. That's what matters. There are many areas of overlap between these pathways, as reflected in various practices. And all routes lead to the same awakening.

THE PRIMARY PATHS

The path of Knowledge is characterized by the intellect, logic, philosophical and scientific tendencies, and self inquiry. The focus is internal and mind centered. The direction is also inward, turning the mind on itself and directing the faculties of the intellect toward understanding one's internal experience. Its purest form is logical self-inquiry.

The path of Devotion is characterized by the emotions, love, religious and contemplative tendencies, and the worship of God, or a personal god, guru, or savior. The focus is internal and heart centered. The direction, however, is outward, toward the object of loving devotion. Its purest forms are devotional service, ritual worship, and surrender of the self to a higher power.

The path of Action is characterized by compassion, practical and sociable tendencies, charity, and kindness to others. The focus is external and on practical matters. The direction is outward toward helping others. Its purest forms are cultivating and practicing loving kindness, contributing to social welfare, and selfless charity for others.

The path of Skill is characterized by creative and aesthetic tendencies, and the cultivation of physical aptitude, health, and manifest beauty. The focus is external and on the body. The direction is inward, however, toward self mastery and personal development. Its purest forms are techniques and practices aimed at control, improvement, and expression of the body-mind, such as postural yoga, martial arts, dance, breath practices, and so on.

INTEGRATED PATHWAYS

The primary pathways represent idealized forms. Generally, all practices, and certainly all practices when put into practice by a person, integrate various aspects of the four pathways. By considering the dominant aspects of various practices, we can approximate their position on the mandala.

Meditation, for example, combines the internal, mind-centered aspects of the Knowledge path with the physical, technique-oriented aspects of the Skill path. Contemplation combines the mind-centered aspects of the Knowledge path with the outward direction of the Devotion path.

When devotional attention is combined with the practical and compassionate regard of the Action path, the result is supplication through prayer. When combining practical and compassionate regard with the Skill path, the result is association with a community of spiritual practitioners.

Combining the Knowledge path with the Action path could result in mindfulness and kindness in everyday activity. Combining the Devotion path with the Skill path could result in renunciation or asceticism. There are many possibilities for combining aspects of the various pathways. Even the primary pathways are constantly integrating aspects of the other paths.

Of course, traps abound everywhere. Wrong views, self righteousness, obsession with gaining personal power, fixation on experiences, and so on also appear everywhere across the mandala. All these traps are obstacles on the path, distorting practices, reinforcing delusions, and diverting spiritual seekers from discovery of the truth.

What the mandala shows, however, is that whatever your background or tendencies, you are *already* on the path, and there are practices to focus your efforts and aid you on your spiritual journey. It is not a question of finding the right religion, the right philosophy, the right technique, or even the right teacher. It is a matter of engaging with the spiritual journey and in the practices and teachers that appear in the context of your life.

Path and Mode

The Path Mandala can be overlaid on the Modes of Practice diagram, with each rotating freely. In this configuration, we can see that any type of practice, wherever it appears on the Path Mandala, will pass through aspects of the four modes: Focusing, Observing, Manipulating, and Emptying. In this way, any practice can be understood as having aspects of path and mode.

Why is this useful?

First, this combined mandala allows us to see the vast array of traditions and practices in a single light, as coexisting opportunities for engaging with the spiritual journey. It allows us to see followers of all the world's religions, cultures, and traditions, old and new, whatever their outward form, as members of a great spiritual community. It allows us to see a Sunday Catholic, a science-minded atheist, a Muslim cleric, an arm-chair philosopher, and a tribal shaman as treading the same path. However the journey manifests in a particular life, we are all destined for the same awakening. And we all face similar challenges, delusions, traps, and setbacks along the way. It allows us to see all beings without discrimination, with equanimity, and with compassion.

Second, the mandala provides the opportunity to reflect upon our own tendencies and our own spiritual journey. Our circumstances and situations have led us to certain practices and patterns of thought that may or may not seem spiritual in nature, and which may or may not suit our outlook, our tendencies, or our current inclinations. The mandala can show us where we are with regard to our practice and guide us toward other areas to explore. There may be a realm of practice we feel drawn to, or that for one reason or another, we feel we must pursue.

Third, by providing conceptual maps for path and mode, the mandala provides opportunities for productive discourse regarding spiritual practice. Skillful application of the maps may even prove useful in diagnosing spiritual obstacles and identifying beneficial practices for overcoming them. For example, we have already pointed out how Focusing practices need to be balanced by Observing practices, and how Manipulating practices need to be balanced by Emptying practices. Many similar directions may be revealed through a careful study of the mandala.

Although the mandala is only a conceptual map, such maps, like various books and teachings, can play an important role in the spiritual journey. Like all maps, they reveal the landscape in a way that can be grasped. In the end, all maps fail in the face of the ungraspable truth, but until then, the mandala can orient us on our quest and help direct our efforts. In other words, it is a signpost, pointing toward awakening.

8

AWARENESS OF BEING

Consciousness itself is the beginning and the end,
the gateway and the goal.

THE ESSENCE OF EXISTENCE

Whatever views you hold or whatever practices you undertake, it should be clear already that *something* is happening. That much we can all generally agree upon. The ideas about what exactly is happening, however, are incredibly diverse. And the debate about how to describe what is happening has itself been happening for a very long time … or so it seems. A brief survey of philosophies and religions — and science too — shows clearly that descriptions of life, the universe, and everything vary widely and are continuously changing. But few, if any, deny that something is happening. Even the nihilist, who rejects that existence has any meaning, has a hard time denying the essence of existence itself.

Of course, some may argue that no concrete objects exist, but none can argue that absolutely nothing is happening. The very argument betrays itself.

Something *is* happening. The question is, what? What is really happening? What is it that we are experiencing? Who exactly is experiencing it? And how do we get to these answers?

If we start to debate — asking if it is a who or a what, or what components does it have, what qualities does it possess, what do the scriptures say, what do the experiments say — then we go down the same old path of subscribing to or creating a model, a concept, an idea of what is. As we have seen, that has been happening for a while already without any end or satisfaction, and there is no reason to suppose it won't continue without any end or satisfaction.

Are we not missing the point? Here we are. *This* is what's happening. This is what is. So in some sense, the answers should lie in plain sight.

In other words, if we are looking to devise self-consistent and workable models, complex relatable ideas, or fantastically convincing dreams, that is one thing, but if we are looking to get to the heart of the matter — truth — that is another thing entirely. To seek the former, we need only keep the awareness on the mind's activity. To seek the latter, we need to see through the mind entirely, and turn awareness on itself, for that is where it is all happening.

So even to ask what is happening may be asking too much. It should be quite obvious that *this* is happening, exactly what is before you now.

We usually have so many thoughts, ideas, speculations, hopes, fears, and desires about *what* exists that we ignore the essence of existence itself.

That essence is the awareness of being. It is the enigmatic *I* behind the thought "I am." We think we are a particular thing, but if we look for it, the thought vanishes. What we thought we were — the ego, mind or body — turns out to be nothing at all, but what remains is the one true Self.

What is Really Happening

The experience we are having right now is all we can ever say is really happening. Everything else is hearsay or inference, fantasy or confabulation — all imaginings, which are occurring here and now.

Sure, we might say they are good inferences. When we look out on the world, based on experience and the apparent repetition of various experiences, we might surmise that such-and-such seems to be the case. We might say that our ability to replicate our experiences and create functional objects based on our ideas proves we are on the right track. But strictly speaking, it does not prove that. One can have a completely imaginary and yet functional idea. In fact, one can have a whole series of ideas and create a wide range of functions without ever seeing the truth.

We can refer to the principle of mathematical equivalence to see that this is so. For any given system, it is possible to create different, yet equally valid and functional mathematical descriptions. In such a case, which one would be right? Of course, this applies to language as well. All descriptions and explanations rely on concepts and metaphor, which always rely on other concepts and metaphors to derive their meaning. Competing explanations could provide equal repeatability and functionality and yet be very different.

Of course, one may argue that further experiments will determine which one is right and so progress is made. But consider carefully the nature of such progress. What one is making progress toward is just a different, more nuanced, more complex, or more simple explanation or mathematical model. But confusion will always arise from mistaking our concepts and explanations about the content of our experience for the experience itself, or from mistaking our idea of reality for reality itself.

Usually, we are starting with and working from an already heavily-conditioned mind. The practical uses of observations, experiments, explanations, descriptions, and mathematical models are clear, and their functionality is self-evident. But without making any prior assumptions, and without relying on any relative concepts or metaphors, do they tell us what's really happening? Is our lack of knowledge simply due to lack of accumulation, or are we fundamentally looking in the wrong place, creating ignorance where none really exists?

If the experience we are having is all we can rely on, perhaps instead of focusing on the contents of that experience, we might gain insight by examining experience itself. Who is having the experience? What is it that we are actually aware of? *That* is what is really happening.

In All Possible States

In our experience, we pass through many states: happiness, sadness, hunger, longing, grief, joy, dissatisfaction, anger, despair, and so on. There is seemingly no end to the number of possible states. In general, when people are seeking, they feel that they are seeking a better state. Perhaps the person wishes to be happier, more fulfilled, more knowledgeable, or even enlightened. While seeking, people always desire a different state, and the spiritually-minded person has in mind an ultimate state, a state of salvation or liberation. This is what the search looks like for the seeker.

While in a manner of speaking, this all may be fine in the beginning, ultimately it is misguided. This business of seeking new, better, and different states is an example of our confusion and the need for clarification. For one cannot experience any state in the future. The only state that can ever be experienced is the one happening now. And any ultimate state cannot sit at the top of a hierarchy of preferable states, but must stand outside of any distinction, eternally encompassing any state that arises. In other words, it cannot be a state, but rather, must be that which underlies all states.

Ordinary states come and go as experiences. Whatever state arises, it will eventually subside. We know this from experience, but it is worthwhile to verify it by observing states as they arise and subside. After all, what are we talking about? Ordinary states are just collections of thoughts, emotions, and sensations. All these things are ephemeral and impermanent. Just observe and see how they come and go. If we are seeking what is eternally true, it cannot be composed of these things. Instead, let us ask: What underlies all these things? What is always present in every possible state?

We might conclude that it is the ego, the mind, or the body itself that underlies all these states. Being identified with the body, we may think that without the body there are no states, and without the mind or ego there would be no experience of them. But these conclusions, which might seem right at first glance, are premature, arising from conditioned thoughts and identification with the ego, mind, and body. For if we examine the breadth of our experience directly, we will discover states in which ego, mind, and/or body are not present. So these also come and go. They are themselves states of being.

There are far too many states, including so-called extraordinary states, to discuss them all individually. So let us go into the heart of the matter by discussing some overarching states everyone is familiar with: waking, dreaming, and deep sleep. These are the broad states which we view as composing our day-to-day life as they come and go, and into which we categorize most of our experiences. For example, if we have an extraordinary experience, we may try to discern whether we were awake or dreaming, even if the experience does not conform to our usual experience of waking or dreaming.

All the states previously mentioned, such as happiness, hunger, desire, anger, et cetera, can be experienced in the waking and dreaming states, but not in deep sleep. We must stir from deep sleep in order for such states to arise. And although we may discern waking and dreaming states in which we are not aware of the mind and/or the body, we know from experience that we are not aware of them in deep sleep. Again, we must stir from deep sleep in order for mind and body to arise within our awareness. As soon as we become aware of these things, we know that we are no longer in the depths of sleep.

From this we know that not only are all the ordinary and overarching states impermanent, but also that in our direct experience, mind and body are impermanent as well, disappearing and appearing, at the very least, with the coming and going of deep sleep. And perhaps we can see now that in our direct experience, the entire world and everything in it also disappears in the depths of sleep. So it too comes and goes, appearing and disappearing from our awareness.

Every state we can think of, including deep sleep, comes and goes. And everything we can think of also comes and goes, as evidenced at least by deep sleep, when all our thoughts disappear. But what is always there, in every imaginable state? What is always there — even in deep sleep — when the mind and body and world have all disappeared?

What is the reality present in all possible states?

NON-CONCEPTUAL EXPERIENCE

We are entranced by objects, events, body and mind. Through conditioning, we construct our identities out of *things,* rooting our sense of being in various conceptual experiences. But that is not the whole of being. That is a limited being, bound by concepts and beliefs about what is happening. Because we are biased toward these things and identify with them, we take our conceptual experience of them to be reality. Anything outside of that, we therefore consider not real or interpret as a conceptual nothing, or a non-experience.

Again, we can use the state of deep sleep as an example, because it removes so many of the things we identify with. Many people will say they have no experience in deep sleep. They will so strongly deny the experience of deep sleep that I hesitate to use this line of thinking. But the reason we don't think we experience deep sleep is precisely because of ego-mind-body identification, as well as various beliefs about time, space, and the world. Since all these are absent in deep sleep, we don't think there is any experience. Yet we will say we enjoy sleeping or that we slept well. When pressed to describe it, we may say it is like an interval of nothing, a dark emptiness, or a blank. But who or what experiences the nothing? We did not question it while asleep. How do we know what it is like, even vaguely? How is it we can say we slept well? Is it just nonsense to say so?

The fact is, we equate experience with experience of *something,* be it an object, a thought, a sensation, or an emotion. We always think in these terms. If we identify with the ego, of course we say sleep is a non-experience because the ego cannot experience it, nor are there *things* to experience in that state. To protect the ego is one of the reasons we so strongly resist the idea of awareness within deep sleep. Consider that even in the waking state, awareness of objects, thoughts, sensations, and so on come and go. Even the ego comes and goes. But we only count those things which we identify with and when they appear. We do not count the intervals in which those things are absent. Instead, we ignore them. We leave them out or fill them in with confabulation.

If we are seeking the unbound totality of being, we cannot leave anything out. And yet, while focused on the conceptual experiences, we leave out the non-conceptual experience. While focused on things, we leave out nothing. While focused on the waking state, we leave out deep sleep. In truth, the distinctions between states is all an illusion. It is simply the coming and going of various things. And if we can experience the absence of one thing, why not the absence of all things?

Deep sleep can be seen as a window into this non-conceptual experience. Awareness persists without subject or objects, without time or space. Similar states are possible in deep meditation. It is precisely because of the absence of a subject or objects, concepts and things, time and space, that such states are indescribable. Ultimately, when one awakens to the unbound totality of being, this non-conceptual experience is present even in the waking state, for consciousness itself, without any subject or objects, is that which underlies all states.

Why bother with all this talk of sleep though? It is only a memory of an idea. Are you sleeping now? When you are asleep, you are silent, and it is clear. Only now, when you are awake, is it a mystery to be solved. For what is asleep while sleeping is awake while waking. And what is awake while sleeping is asleep while waking. So let us instead look to that which is awake while sleeping and waking — dreaming too!

Being and Nonbeing

Relative, conceptual being is limited, but absolute being is beyond both being and non-being, which are only concepts. This is not just a word game, nor is it merely a spiritual platitude pointing toward something greater than our individual lives, toward that which is eternal, unborn, undying, and unchanging. It is not a philosophy. It is not itself a concept to be believed or disbelieved. It is the reality in which we exist. And this absolute being can be recognized, experienced, and known without doubt.

For the purposes of thought and discussion, we can entertain concepts of being and non-being, existence and non-existence. But when all the thoughts have run their course, we will still be no closer to the truth. When the discussion has died down, we will still have no definitive answer to the mystery of our lives. Fixated on a limited view of existence as an ego-self contained within a body, we may wait for the next thought or the next discussion to arise. And with each thought and each discussion, we hope for some satisfaction, some clarity, that never seems to arrive.

Is there any other way? How can we recognize this absolute being?

It cannot be touched by concepts and ideas, which are always bound by dualistic views. It cannot be grasped by the ego, which is itself only an idea or collection of ideas. All words go dark in the light of its presence. And yet, it is so close, so intimate and immediate. We can ignore it, but we cannot really escape it. For this absolute being is actually our own being.

Instead of engaging the mind with concepts and ideas, quiet the mind and allow innate awareness to encompass everything. Within this awareness, there is no inside or outside, no being or non-being, no life or death, no self or other, no body or world. There is just Being. It is like a vast emptiness, and yet, ten thousand suns could not be brighter than its darkness.

9

THE TOTAL ENVIRONMENT

Nothing can be outside of everything.

ARGUMENTS ALONE
WILL NOT SUFFICE

If we pursue the spiritual journey consciously and with some intellectual vigor, we are likely to run into or to come up with all kinds of interesting philosophical, theological, scientific, and a few just plain wacky ideas and arguments. Some are meticulously crafted with scholarly methods and strict adherence to logic. Some have evolved and been passed down through cultural traditions. Others are less rigorous, more off-the-cuff explanations than carefully constructed arguments.

Whatever the case, all such arguments can be a maze of confusion. Many people seek out argument after argument, as strikes their fancy, and with each new argument, they will remodel the entire universe. We can become intoxicated by such power, drunk with our ability to understand the world anew. But with each new argument and model the mind grabs hold of, we become more entangled in the web of our dreams. We think we will eventually find the right argument, the right model, but at best, all we ever find are brief distractions from the steady stream of our confusion.

Nevertheless, in this book you encounter a variety of arguments. To some extent they are philosophical and logical, and in some cases they reflect traditional arguments, but it would be a lie to say they are meticulously crafted. In that sense, they are more the off-the-cuff type. Some may even seem a bit wacky from a conventional point of view. But they are born from clear insight, and their real purpose is not to convince you of anything anyway, but instead to cast doubt upon your current views, to open the mind and thereby lead you to inquiry.

These arguments would seem to lend themselves to a new model of the world, or to confirm a model you already have. But to take them that way would be a mistake with regard to your spiritual journey. Some arguments do point more directly toward the truth than others, but they are still not the truth themselves. So let me be very clear. Any arguments contained herein are not presented as an outline for a new conceptual worldview. I can't stress that enough. This is such a common mistake — one that I made for years — and it never leads to satisfaction. No conceptual worldview will ever satisfy our inmost longing to directly experience what is.

The arguments contained herein are seeds for deep spiritual inquiry. If you find them compelling, it's okay to have some faith in what I'm saying, but only on the way to your own inquiry. Our faith should give us courage to look deeper. The spiritual journey progresses when we look into things and discover for ourselves what is really true and what is not. So don't make the mistake of taking any argument, concept, or worldview as reality. Don't take anybody's words for the truth — not even your own.

WE CANNOT STAND APART FROM REALITY

Let's face it, reality being reality — whatever it is — there is no way we can stand apart from it. This may seem too obvious to point out, but if we examine the way we view ourselves and the world, it's clear that we often treat ourselves as if we are separate and apart from the reality in which we exist. We imagine a division between subject and object. Our idea of reality is the objective world. But our idea of ourselves is as a subject looking at the world, as if we existed outside of it. But how is this possible? Reality encompasses everything that is, so subject and object must share one and the same reality.

It's very difficult to really get at what I'm talking about here, because language itself models the view of separate subjects and objects. Don't make this more complicated than it is, but also don't dismiss it out of hand. Intellectual understanding is not enough. If you can really see this, the implications are profound. What you think to be your self, becomes just another object appearing in reality. The true subject is revealed as reality itself, and all the objects appearing in it are revealed as nothing but that. Suddenly, a kind of total perception opens up, a perception without any divisions, and which leaves nothing out.

It cannot actually be explained in such a way that one will really get it. By getting it intellectually, we may actually lose it. For it is not a matter of grasping on to a new conceptual object, but rather of seeing the subject as just another conceptual object. It is not a matter of experiencing the world as reality through the ego-self, but rather a matter of experiencing reality as reality through reality. We think we are that which *gets,* that which acquires new concepts. But all concepts are only concepts, and all thoughts are only thoughts. So there is no one to get them. The reality is already the reality. It cannot gain anything, for it is already complete. It needs no new understanding, for it is not ignorant of anything.

Confused? Okay, fair enough. In trying to explain the unexplainable, I admit that things can get a little out of hand. Let's slow down and work toward it from a different angle. It's worth the effort, because sometimes, when hearing about it for the umpteenth time, one will just let go, and then it appears. Then there's a chance to *really* get it … or lose it … or however we're going to not quite say it.

The main thing is, we are *in* reality. It's radical, I know, but it's hard to deny so it's a good point to hammer on. Whatever this is, it is or is a part of reality. And being a part of reality really just means, without limits, it *is* reality. If we wonder where we come from, or how the mind appears, we need look no further than reality. If we came from somewhere else, that too would be a part of reality. And whatever part we are looking at, it is just reality.

Nevertheless, in our myths and in our everyday views, we conceive of ourselves as coming into this world from someplace else, or of peering at it from the dark vaults of the mind, or of being trapped in a body. The ego-self is conceived as being this separate entity. But how could we come *into* reality from somewhere else, when everyplace is reality? A tree grows out of the total environment, and is a part of it. Like this, we grow out of reality, and also are a part of it. So wherever and whatever we imagine ourselves to be, and whenever we look for something other to explain this situation, there is actually nothing but reality itself.

There are no Objects
or Events

Discreet objects and events are the stuff of the everyday world, and the stuff of the language with which we make sense of it. They are the stuff of history, the stuff of galaxies, and the stuff of people. How, then, can it make any sense to say there are no objects or events?

Objects and events are relative terms for impermanent phenomena, defined by thought-created limits. With regard to absolute reality, there is only what is — the total environment. So while within it, there may be objects and events, galaxies and people, actually there isn't. There is nothing but reality itself.

Ask yourself, in your experience, what makes an object an object? Examine this very closely. Do we see something separate, and then the mind draws distinctions? Or does the mind draw distinctions, and then we see something separate? When distinctions are made, edges are formed, limits are established, thoughts arise, various sensations are correlated, and an idea is formed of the object as separate from ourselves and the rest of the world. It is only then that we can talk about it as an object, a jar for instance, or a book, and its relationship to other objects, like a table or your hand. We think objects are already there, but in our actual experience, they only come into our awareness through mind activity. Ask yourself, in your direct experience, is an object an object when you do not perceive it *as* an object. What is it when you are not perceiving it or thinking about it as an object?

We can make the same inquiry for events as we do for objects. It makes sense to do so because we can gain insights into each by examining the other. The limitations of an event are temporal. Objects could even be seen as a particular type of event. They appear and disappear, arise and subside, come into being and go out of being. Each event has a beginning and an end. But these beginnings and endings, like the spatial boundaries of an object, only come into being through mind activity. All events, like all objects, are thought created, for without thoughts, there is no beginning and no end … no limit.

Without any real limits, there are no objects or events. There is just the total environment.

We might say the total environment is a single object, the only object in existence. But who is experiencing it? And what is outside of it? We might say it is one grand event, apart from which nothing has happened. But who has taken notice? And where does it begin and end? In fact, the total environment cannot be an object or event, precisely because it has no limit.

When we try to encompass this total environment with the mind, we are dumbfounded, because the mind itself is an object within it, with each successive thought, an event that comes and goes. And as we have seen, there really aren't any objects or events.

There is no Inside or Outside

Typically, we think of ourselves as existing inside a body and mind, and that outside of us is the world in which our body and mind exist. But there is really no inside or outside to the situation. Outside is always just the things you don't think of as inside. And inside is always just the things you don't think of as outside. Furthermore, the boundary between them is mutable and ever-changing. Regarding the totality of *what is,* you will never find anything that is outside of it, and you will never find anything that is not inside of it.

Inside and outside, the way we think about them, are only thoughts. They are relative terms, used to discuss various relationships between objects and their thought-created boundaries. Without boundaries, there can be no inside or outside. The terms become meaningless. So the first thing to see is that all the limits and boundaries we place on things have no reality aside from the thoughts themselves.

For example, we may say the skin is the boundary of the body, and at a certain level of magnification it makes sense. But is it really a boundary at all? If we think about the fundamental stuff of the skin, it is the same kind of fundamental stuff that exists outside of it. We might say empty space mostly, as well as some protons, neutrons, electrons, and so on. Maybe the density and arrangement of these things change, but they are constantly changing, and at a high-enough level of magnification, there is mostly just empty space. At what point can any real boundary be said to exist?

We might say the limits of the mind are clear. We cannot know what's going on right now on the other side of the universe, or even in the next room. We cannot know what we do not experience. But not having experienced something, there is nothing to not know. In other words, can the mind really *not know* anything? It can experience, make distinctions, analyze relationships, and create models. But we can never be aware of anything we do not know. The moment we become aware of it, it is known. Before that, there is nothing to know or not know.

We imagine that we are inside our bodies and minds, looking out at the world, but where is this body and mind if not *in* the world we are looking at? And where is this image that appears as the world, if not *in* the mind. This being the situation, how can there be any inside or outside?

There is no Space or Time

The essence of these arguments is to show that what we think of as reality is only a function of what we call mind, and that this mind does not exist. Whatever remains is reality itself, without objects or events, without an inside or an outside … and without space or time, for even these, when examined closely, are also functions of mind.

Some people will surely reject this out of hand as nonsense. Some others may say "Duuude, you're so right!" But either reaction is problematic. Like all these arguments, our inquiry is what really matters. Just rejecting or accepting any argument is not enough. You have to really check it out deeply. Don't take that lightly, either. I mean break-your-mind-on-it deep. Even then you won't reach any conclusion, but in the aftermath of that kind of inquiry, the truth may suddenly appear.

When you stand in the middle of a vast plain and look out at the horizon, you may think the horizon is far away. But what do you really see? Nothing but a line, arcing in a circle all around you.

As you walk, the horizon in front recedes away from you, so that you will never reach it. The horizon behind follows you, but will never catch up.

At some point you might see a green smudge on the horizon ahead of you. As you walk, it gets bigger. Eventually you see a tree. The tree gets bigger and bigger until it towers above you. You may think that a tree in the distance got closer and closer until you were standing in front of it. But what is your actual experience? A green smudge got bigger until you saw a tree. Then the tree got bigger until it filled your view.

The horizon is always the horizon. Green smudges are always green smudges. And trees are always trees. Nothing can be farther away. Nothing can be closer. Space is always space, and yet, when we walk, we do not *move* through it. So what space is there? When you dream, a whole world appears, and yet there is nowhere to go. When you awake from your dream, all that space disappears, and there is still nowhere to go.

On an autumn evening you sit and watch some birds fly south. They appear in the north, pass over head, and disappear beyond the horizon. You stare at the empty sky and think about what has really happened. The birds are gone already, but the moment has never passed. Now their passing is only a memory, but you cannot be sure they were really there. You wonder where they are off to, but they have already left. You imagine in the spring they will return, but it's not even winter, and the autumn sky is as vast as your imagination.

It always has been, and always will be now. Everything that has ever happened has happened now, and everything that ever will happen will also happen now. The past, as we remember it, is already gone. It has never been the past. And the future, as we imagine it, will never really arrive. Whatever you do, you will always be doing it now. Even when you are lost in memory, you are lost in present memory. Even when you dream of the future, you are dreaming now. There is no past or future. There is no time. This present moment is all there ever really is.

10

ENDING ALL CONFLICT

In the realm of what is, there are no obstructions.

GOING INTO FEAR AND DESIRE

When we consciously set out on a spiritual path, we do so with many ideas, assumptions, and fantasies about what we're doing and where it's all going. The actual path is simply the falling away of ideas, assumptions, and fantasies. But at the beginning, we have these things as part of the makeup of the ego. Everything we experience is experienced through the viewpoint of this ego, and we really don't know where it's all going.

If our intentions are sincere, we may begin to question everything, to inquire into every aspect of ourselves, our experience, and the world around us. At the beginning, we hope we will discover something good, something wonderful, something satisfying. But within our sincere practice lies the discovery of our fear, our aggression, our selfishness, our desires, our anger, our arrogance, our ambitions, and our pain.

Soon, what started off as a way to acquire something good, to attain knowledge, or to better ourselves, becomes more a matter of just dealing with ourselves. And we struggle to let go of our fear, our aggression, our selfishness, our desires, and so on. But even that is not enough.

Ultimately, the journey requires letting go of everything all at once, including ourselves. It requires not only an unreserved acceptance of one's life, but also of one's death — not as a future event, but as a present reality, that is always here and now.

The spiritual journey requires complete and profound surrender. It is not a matter of self-improvement, nor of strengthening any personal spirit. Unfortunately for our egos, it's more a matter of letting go of this person, and of recognizing the undifferentiated spirit that is everything and everyone.

So along the path, we should set our intentions beyond ourselves. But to go beyond ourselves, we must go into ourselves. To let go of our fear, our aggression, our selfishness, and so on, we must go into these things and see them for what they are. When we see the incredible tangle that is the ego, freedom is not a matter of casting off individual fears and desires, but rather of seeing through them all together.

The spiritual path turns everything on its head. To free ourselves of fear, we cannot push fear away. We must instead go right into the very heart of our fear, into that which we fear the most, and see clearly what it is we are really afraid of. To free ourselves from desire, we cannot avoid desire. Without any action, we must instead go into the root of our desire and see clearly that satisfaction is always present, always with us, here and now.

In the end, we do not free ourselves of fear and desire by letting go of fear and desire, but rather, by letting go of ourselves.

Cultivating Love and Compassion

The spiritual community is replete with advice on being more loving and compassionate. So on the path, we may seek to grow in this regard. It sounds like a great plan, but how do we do it?

Love has a thousand ears and a thousand hearts, but they are not *our* ears, and they are not *our* hearts. Compassion has a thousand eyes and a thousand hands, but they are not *our* eyes, and they are not *our* hands. However, when our ears are not our ears and our hearts are not our hearts, when our eyes are not our eyes and our hands are not our hands, then love and compassion has our ears and our hearts, our eyes and our hands.

What can it possibly mean?

It means we cannot *make* ourselves more loving and compassionate. We can only give up our selves. When selfishness falls away, love and compassion take care of everything, without discrimination.

Of course we should try, by doing what we think and feel is loving or what we believe and feel is compassionate. However hard we try, though, as long as we are trying to improve ourselves, as long as we think love and compassion is something that can be increased or gained, we will never really expand our love and compassion. But if we forsake ourselves, give up our interests, let go of our hopes, and make friends with our fears, then something else entirely can come into our lives. For behind the illusion of the self, love is like an ocean which has no beginning or end, no bottom, no surface, and no shore. And compassion is the ever-present and inescapable truth itself.

Whatever love we enjoy, whatever compassion we show, we have by grace, for it is not created by our egos. It is ever-present, before all our conditioned thoughts and dreams, hopes and fears. What we enjoy, what we show, is the infinite light that shines through the fragmented armor of the ego, and it is often distorted, refracting off the hard edges of the gaps it shines through.

In this sense, "cultivating love and compassion" could be a misleading phrase. Perhaps we could say, *unveiling* or *discovering* love and compassion. And we do this by simply letting go of the self, by dismantling the ego, by taking off our armor. When you breath in, inhale into the tensions that hold this armor together, and you will inhale all the troubles of the world. When you breath out, release these bonds, exhaling freely, and you will exhale love and compassion.

Just do this, in whatever circumstances arise, and you may find the love that is ever present. It is not *your* love, but it is a love far greater than you can imagine, and it's shining through you.

Embracing Equanimity

On the spiritual journey, as in all journeys, there are many ups and downs. Sometimes we may feel good about ourselves and the world. Everything is going really well. We are making progress toward our goals. Things are making sense. Other times we may feel bad about ourselves and the world. The situation seems hopeless. Our goals seem unreachable. We are more confused than ever. Occasionally we may feel ecstatic, filled with manifestations of love, joy, or awe. Occasionally we may also feel depressed. Life itself may seem pointless, troublesome, or to be a source of unmitigated and endless suffering.

These are the very ups and downs of life. Day to day, month to month, year to year, we are subjected to the desperation of hope, the exhilaration of success, the joys of romantic love, the catastrophic grief of mourning, the nagging of frustration, and so much more. We are tied to these ups and downs as one bound to the wheel of samsara. Wrapped up in this roller coaster of highs, lows, and everything in between, our view is very limited. We identify with our states, and are blind to what lies beyond them. So when we are up we rejoice, and when we are down we wail.

In general, we tend to seek out the ups and try to avoid the downs. We seek out pleasure and try to avoid pain, on many different levels and in many different ways. Even if we see logically that good and bad must arise mutually — that you can't have one without the other — we cannot help it. We want to be happy, we want good things, pleasurable experiences, desired outcomes. We do not want any unpleasantness, although sometimes we see it as necessary for some greater good. "Fine," we say, "that's all right, as long we keep the greater good in mind."

Nobody would want unmitigated, unrelenting, unending pain. That would be the ultimate bad — basically hell. And yet, when we set out upon our journey, we seem to be seeking the ultimate good, a state of permanent happiness — salvation or heaven. What's wrong with that? Well … just that it's not what you think. If you chase after that kind of heaven, you will never reach it, and hell will always be at your heels. For the ultimate good and the ultimate bad also arise mutually. The real heaven is beyond all our ideas of heaven and hell.

What has never begun and never ended, reality itself, alone endures. All things are impermanent, for whatever arises must pass away, and whatever is born must die. That is the way of things. Inquire into anything and see the truth of it. Watch carefully and you will see clearly, when things are great it never lasts, and when things are terrible it never lasts either. Everything changes. There is no stopping it and nothing to hang on to.

If we can see even a glimmer of the impermanence of all things, it's time we take seriously the prospect that we may have been looking in the wrong direction. If you have been holding out hope that you will get something good out of this spiritual quest, that your ego will be rewarded in some way, that you will acquire something you do not have, if you have been searching for your idea of heaven, if you have been running away from anything or thinking you can escape from something, especially your fears, your search has led you astray. The truth alone is unrelentingly real, and it contains all things — the ups, the downs, and everything in between.

This truth is always with us. We cannot catch it, nor can we escape from it. For it is never actually apart from us. That it seems apart is only an illusion created by ignorance. So if we chase after it, it will seem to recede from us. If we try to escape from it, it will seem to follow us. But never, for even a moment, has it ever been absent or apart from us.

In light of this, we can endeavor to take everything into ourselves, approaching whatever arises with a spirit of equanimity. By widening the expanse of our awareness, we can see the ups and the downs together, and by recognizing impermanence we can accept everything. We need not desire the ups, for they come of their own accord. We need not despise the downs, for they too arise naturally. We can let go of the drama inherent in the idea of ourselves. We can let go of ourselves, and with equanimity, we can embrace spaciousness, kindness, and compassion in every situation.

RESOLVING CHOICE
AND CHOICELESSNESS

When we go deep into our inquiry, examining thought, emotion, time, action, memory, and so on, we may begin to seriously question ourselves as agents of free will. After all, can we predict what memory we will have, or what thoughts will arise? Do we know our emotions before they appear? Can we say for certain that we will perform an action before we actually perform it? At any moment, in that moment, is there any way we could *not* do what we are doing? And is there ever a time when we are not in this moment now?

Try to catch the moment in which a choice is made. It's not as easy as you might think. We might, for example, choose to raise our hand in the air. We might think, *I'm going to raise my hand in the air,* but that is just a thought that has arisen. Then we may raise the hand. It just goes up. Of course, we might think, *I am choosing to do this,* or *I chose to do it,* but those too are only thoughts arising now. The choice itself is incredibly elusive. If you think you've caught it, ask yourself, from where does it originate? Who or what is choosing? Don't just say "I am" and leave it that. Try to really locate this "I" that is choosing. If you cannot find it, inquire again into the moment of choice.

Sure, ordinarily it seems like we are free agents choosing various paths. However, if we look at things in a particular way, it can start to seem as if everything is on autopilot, as if the whole world and everybody in it, and even our own thoughts, are all automatic mechanisms, simply responding to various laws of cause and effect. This in itself is an interesting insight, but only so far as it challenges previous ideas or views you may have held. The truth is beyond all our ideas, and all our particular views.

The question of free will is only relevant to an idea of the individual ego-self who would possesses or not possess this will, and from a point of view in which some things possess free will while others do not. That is, it is a problem which arises only in relation to certain ideas and points of view. As long as we believe in the agency of the ego-self, the question of whether it has free will or not may trouble us. But if the ego-self is empty — an illusion only — then what is there to possess or not possess this will? The entire question disappears. If all phenomenon can be seen as automatic, then they could also be seen as spontaneously arising, as the limitless Self, and as the will of God. The naked truth has no point of view, and cannot be named, described, categorized, or limited in any way whatsoever.

So if we are to inquire into choice and choicelessness, we should be clear that, ordinarily, one is relative to the other. Ordinary choicelessness is simply no choice. But there is a choicelessness beyond choice and no choice, and that is another matter entirely. The truth could be said to be choiceless in this way, but it is not a matter of lacking choice or lacking free will. It is all encompassing … lacking nothing … completely free. But here, the ego-self and its whole way of approaching the question is revealed as nothing more than illusions created by identification with conditioned thoughts. So choicelessness is reached not by removing choice, but by removing the self who chooses.

Ordinary choice and choicelessness, free will or lack thereof, voluntary and involuntary, inside and outside, self and other, are resolved through realization. All dualities collapse. Concepts and ideas self-destruct. Fundamental groundlessness is revealed. That is, there is nothing to hang to. Nothing can be grasped. There are no choices to be made and nobody to make them. The ego-self goes silent, and in this silence, without effort, everything is taken care of.

Profound Surrender

As we set out upon the path we begin by seeking out our hopes and desires, and running away from our fears and aversions. We may desire some reassurance of safety in a chaotic and dangerous world. We may hope to find something beautiful, something wonderful. We may try to escape from our deepest fears. We may want to fulfill our grand ambitions, build up or confirm our conceptual models, and so on.

But we do not find satisfaction in any of these pursuits. We may pretend to for a time, but in the end we are always disillusioned. Bit by bit, we discover that there is no end to the problems we imagine. And there are no real solutions for them, either. If our hoped for desires are achieved, more desires follow. If our fears are averted, more fears arise. Our conflicts with ourselves, with others, and with the world persist, as does our suffering — big and small.

If we are sincere in our efforts, we will look squarely and critically at our hopes and fears, our desires and aversions. Through practice, we will try to manage them. We will let go of the ones we can, and we will negotiate with the ones we can't, mitigating their hold over us and the suffering they cause. We will find clever ways to deal with them, to work around them, and to lessen the burden on ourselves and others. We will cultivate our ability to endure them with equanimity, and we will discover whatever love and compassion shines through the armor of our egos. But still, we will not be free.

We cannot give up in our quest. If we are honest with ourselves, courageous in our inquiry, we may begin to see that the difficulty lies not with the things we desire or fear, nor even with desire and fear themselves. The issue is not with the situation as it presents itself, as an arrangement of subjects and objects, people and events, but rather with the fundamental situation itself. It is a question of our very existence.

Through grace, we may truly surrender some of our hopes and fears. We may go on with our practice and our journey. We may forgive. We may be redeemed. We may bear our grief. We may endure our pains and find humility in our suffering. But the ego remains, and there will always be more to surrender until everything is surrendered at once.

One way or another, if followed, the spiritual journey leads to a truly profound surrender. Really, it is not even enough to say complete surrender, for we might imagine there is still a person to surrender completely. Profound surrender is not just letting go of safety, hopes, fears, ambitions, concepts, and so on. It is totally letting go of one's self. It is a kind of death, and the end of the ego-self. It is the realization that there is nothing to let go of. It is a mystery. It is the harbinger of awakening. It the herald of enlightenment.

PART III

THE SILENCE

11

CRISIS AND AWAKENING

The ego-self and all conceptual frameworks come to an end.

UNIVERSAL INQUIRY

The true teaching is simply disillusionment. It does not give you anything. Instead, it pulls the rug out from under you. It prompts you to drop all your concepts and beliefs. Most of us have had at least a limited experience of this. We think things are a certain way, and then realize we were mistaken, that the way we thought things were was wrong. Suddenly we drop what we see as a wrong view. Usually, however, we instantly replace it with another view — a new idea, a new concept, or a new belief. Our tendency is to avoid experiencing emptiness. For total disillusionment, we have to drop everything all at once, without picking up anything new.

The true practice is simply letting go. It also gives you nothing. Instead, it shows you everything you're holding on to and demands you let go of it all. We are prompted to let go of ingrained patterns of physical and psychological tension, to let go of our thoughts, to let go of the endless stories we tell about ourselves, to let go of our conditioned ideas, our unfounded beliefs, our selfish desires, our grandiose ambitions, our nagging restlessness, our righteous indignation, our need to be right, our false piety, and on and on and on. Again, we've all probably had some limited experience of this, some relief we have felt from the dropping away of an attachment. But through practice, we see just how deep it goes and how attachment works through a cycle of identification. To totally let go, the cycle itself must be broken.

So the spiritual journey progresses from looking at individual thoughts, ideas, and beliefs to looking at the whole of the mind. And it progresses from letting go of individual attachments to letting go of the whole cycle of identification and attachment. This is important. Letting go of individual things is not the point. That can be helpful in terms of clarification and as a catalyst for inquiry, but ultimately we must question everything. It is not enough to question a particular thought if we do not question thought itself. It is not enough to question a particular object if we do not question time and space itself. It is not enough to question the particular contents of the mind if we do not question the mind itself. And it is not enough to question particular aspects of ourselves if we do not question the very nature of our selves.

By questioning everything, our journey leads to an inquiry into the most fundamental nature of our experience. Each thing we question leads to more underlying questions, until we arrive at the most basic and challenging questions.

What is the world? What is reality? What is the mind? What is consciousness? What is God?

Why is there suffering?

What is really happening?

What am I? Where am I? Who am I?

There are no easy answers to these questions when asked with sincerity. Each answer that arises must be carefully evaluated to see if any further question or doubt remains, or if anything has been left out. When evaluated this way, all such answers will be discarded, for the mind itself is also an object of inquiry, as is the one who is asking the question. Therefore, questions will always remain. To discover the mystery of our true nature, we must go beyond the mind and beyond the questioner. Only there will we reach the end of our inquiry.

BREAKDOWN OF REASON

The relentless pursuit of the truth through any practice, such as inquiry or meditation, prayer or devotion, via any path, always leads to a kind of breakdown. This is actually a sign of progress — the time to really pay attention. The conceptual structures that support our methods are strained to the breaking point and can no longer be maintained. Reason itself begins to break down.

This can manifest in a number of ways. In the case of inquiry, it may feel like there is no place else to go, nothing further to explore, no more leads, no more answers. In the case of meditation or some physical practice, it may feel as if there is no point, or the reasons for practice may become utterly mundane or non-existent. In the case of prayer or devotion, one may doubt one's faith, or just have no will to continue. It does not necessarily mean you stop practicing, but all practices may begin to feel empty. All explanations seem inadequate. All concepts seem hollow.

On the spiritual journey, many people may become attached to their questions, their practices, their explanations, their mantras, their prayers, and the trappings of their religion or their outlook. We can become very attached to all these forms. If they begin to falter, we may feel resistance to the change, so let's talk a little bit about why this breakdown must occur.

Truth encompasses everything. It is beyond any particular method. It is beyond any practice, any explanation, any motivation. It is beyond any concept, any philosophy, any religion. So the limitations of any practice, method, or outlook must break down and burn away before the truth can be revealed. Likewise, the truth is always present, and so we have never really been lacking it. Our methods and practices have been both a way to seek the truth *and* a way to hide from it … to prolong our ignorance. After all, how can we seek what is always present? Our very seeking is a form of ignorance. So all our seeking must come to an end.

All that being said, we cannot force this breakdown to come about. It is a *real* breakdown. And we cannot force our seeking to stop. It will just keep happening until we actually come to the end of our seeking. Perhaps the only way to accelerate the process is to engage in the very life and practices that will eventually fall apart. But if we know we are already on the path, and that the path has an end, we can enter into it with the intention and determination to be disillusioned of all our ideas, to let go of ourselves and discover the truth.

When we approach the end of the mind, the end of our seeking, the end of our struggles, or the end of any particular practice, the tendency is to scrabble around for a new line of thinking or a new approach, to find a new practice or a new teacher. Because we are accustomed to basing our decisions on reason and the ego, we may feel monumentally confused, frustrated, stuck, or unable to make decisions. Because we are accustomed to basing our motivations on desire, we may feel listless and without hope or direction. Many times we will redirect ourselves to avoid feeling such emptiness. But a time will come when even that is no longer possible, when reason itself will break down, when desire itself will burn out, and we will have no choice but to gaze into emptiness.

Existential Crisis

All paths, if followed to their ultimate ends, lead to existential crisis. It is inevitable. For who we think we are, what we think the world is, and how we think it all works, are all built up through conditioned thoughts. We have a conceptual view and are having a conceptual experience. But it is, essentially, a house of cards, and with the breakdown of reason, it all teeters at the point of collapse.

Notice how people react when their views are challenged. People hold a wide variety of views. We might say there are as many views as there are people. But when their view of themselves or the world is challenged, in even small ways, they become defensive. They put up their guard. Sometimes they get totally bent out of shape. They may be angry, dismissive, argumentative, or even violent.

Why?

Delusion is built up through layer upon layer of conditioned thoughts, ideas, concepts, and beliefs. When even just the top layers are disturbed, the disruption spreads like a wave through every layer, and the whole structure can be destabilized. Way at the bottom of this structure, the very first layer, supporting it all, is the ego — our idea of an individual and separate self. In this way, a challenge to even minor aspects of our view can be felt as a challenge to our identity, our idea of ourselves, and our very existence. It's no wonder people get bent out of shape.

Just knowing this should engender some worldly compassion, and gives us insight into the spiritual journey. For these very delusions are the source of ignorance, and the only obstacles to awakening. Our inquiry and our practice aims to disturb and dismantle all these layers of conditioning. So all along, this existential crisis has been unavoidable. It is not a matter of everything coming together in the end, but rather of everything falling apart.

When reason breaks down and the structure of our delusions begins to collapse, it is our own existence that is on the line. We may feel the full extent of our existential dread, and we may experience the stark fear of annihilation. But we do not have to resist. We do not have to tighten the straps of our armor. We do not have to redirect ourselves or rebuild our defenses. We can just let go. When emptiness is revealed, we can gaze into it, unhindered by our hopes and our fears. And if we have come to the end of our journey, we can do nothing but that.

Existential Collapse

Our experience of an individual "I" or an ego-self that is distinct and separate from others and from the rest of the world is an illusion created through conditioning. That the world is separate from God and that God is separate from the Self is also an illusion. Before awakening, this can be nothing more than an intellectual understanding or belief. But it can be fully realized. It *is* possible! Not only is it available to all, but it is our destiny — nothing other than our true nature.

But when we finally awaken from our dream, the whole structure of conditioning must come crashing down like the house of cards that it is. This individual self and all its ideas, concepts, and beliefs, must be emptied out and dissolved into nothingness. The cycle of identification and attachment must break, and our limited existence has to collapse, with no hope or question of rebuilding it.

The course of our inner lives comes full circle and finally reaches an end. The ego is exhausted. All its habitual patterns have run their course. Nothing has worked. Nothing has granted satisfaction. There is really nowhere else to go, nothing else to do. Reason breaks down. Attachments fall away. Body and mind drop off. Beliefs and concepts no longer hold. And we can see the world and the totality of our life as emptiness itself.

Distinctions begin to fade. Are we witnessing the world, or are we the world witnessing itself? It is no longer clear. There is no longer a clear dividing line between oneself and the world, between the body and space, between now and eternity, between objects and the vastness of the sky.

We have come to the end, but we have not yet awakened to our true nature. Distinctions have dissolved, but we have not recognized that which is before us. There is no going back, but limitlessness has not been realized. And yet, here we stand at the gate of enlightenment.

Sudden Awakening

We cannot let go of ourselves, but through the grace of profound surrender, everything falls away — mind-body and world, self and other, seeker and goal, life and death, past and future. The grace is ever present, but when the ego-self and all its attachments — its hopes and fears, its desires and dreams, its ambitions and regrets — have been emptied out, profound surrender is possible. From a place of silence, we awaken fully to our true nature. Nothing is left out. And this sudden awakening is liberation, is realization, is enlightenment itself.

While we were on the path, there was plenty of work to do, in which we could make gradual progress. There was room for improvement when it came to our behavior, our outlook, our thoughts, our practices. But when it comes to this ... when it comes to enlightenment, there can be no gradual approach. It is like falling into an abyss. It is like being struck by lightning. It is like the appearance of the sun at dawn. It is like all these, and yet it cannot be described.

Whatever remains of the ego is torn apart. The universe itself turns inside-out, such that inside becomes outside and outside becomes inside. In an instant, all distinctions totally vanish. There is no inside or outside anymore, no near or far, no past or future. What was a great mystery while in the cycle of delusion is now quite obvious, and we might wonder how we could have overlooked so clear a reality. We might wonder, how could we have been so incredibly lost?

Because its very nature is absolute and eternal, because seer, seeing, and seen are inseparable, because time itself falls away with the delusions of the world, awakening dawns with sudden completeness, full of radiant bliss. Total perception reveals itself as nothing other than the kingdom of heaven. How incredible! How wonderful! How beautiful! To be free — truly free — comes as a great surprise, with laughter, tears, bewilderment, joy, and relief beyond imagination.

The individual self is no longer the individual, but is the universe, the truth itself. The universe is no longer the universe, but is the eternal Self. God is no longer God, but is this present experience. And this experience is no longer this experience, but is the omnipresence of the Lord. How can it be described to those still caught in attachments? How can it be explained in dualistic thought? It cannot. But when you are silent it speaks, and when it speaks you are no more. You are only *that*. You always have been, and always will be that.

12

ENLIGHTENMENT REVEALED

Gone beyond — beyond beyond —
where none can say what has happened.

LIMITLESS PERFECTION

Here we come to the place in the book where we attempt the impossible. We will try to describe the indescribable, in an attempt to express the inexpressible, so that you may think the unthinkable. We will, as Douglas Adams put it, "grapple with the ineffable itself, and see if we may not eff it after all."

Let's be very clear, though. It really is an impossible task. Whatever I may say, nothing can truly convey what it's like to have awakened to the truth. For it is not something that can be conveyed. It is direct seeing — total perception — and so we have to see it for ourselves.

Knowing clearly the impossibility of this task, I seriously considered leaving out this section of the book. There are some good reasons to press forward though, even if we can't paint a full picture. For one thing, we have only been pointing all along, so there's no reason not to go on pointing by attempting to go into the experience of awakening itself. More importantly, such a discussion could encourage those who are on the path, and that is no small matter. Of course, there is a risk of fueling egoic desires and deluded ideas, but there is also the opportunity for disillusionment, and that is the teaching itself. So let's go into it a little, keeping in mind the limitations of any explanation or description.

First, let us say that what *is* ... is a limitless perfection, without any boundary whatsoever, and without flaw or flawlessness. Those who have fully awakened have realized their true nature and the nature of the world — of everything and everyone — as that. There is nothing but that. We may call it groundless being. We may call it the Self or God. We may call it Brahman. We may call it Tao. We may call it sunyata, tathata, or dharmakaya. And we may call it by a wide variety of metaphysical terms and by the names of all the gods and goddesses. But all these names point to the limitless One. And because it is one, it is perfect. Because it is one, that's all there is.

This may sound mystical to any individual who has not realized oneness, and it should. Don't make the mistake of thinking enlightenment is some combination of intellectual understanding, accumulated wisdom, or worldly restraint. That is not to disparage these qualities. They are admirable qualities, but of themselves they are not realization — they are not enlightenment. Awakening is awakening. It is nothing other than that. We do not gain anything by it. Instead, it is the end of the individual self, of delusion and ignorance. Everything falls away, and suddenly, *it* is revealed — the great perfection.

What is it like to experience that? Well, there is no separate person to have the experience. It is *that* which is experiencing. This is why it is called the Self and groundless being. Also, there is no separate experience of it. This is why it is called consciousness itself and the eternal. Finally, there is no separate thing to experience. This is why it is called the One and non-dual.

THE END OF ALL THINGS

I once spoke to somebody about the cataclysm of awakening. It's not a particularly cheerful way of explaining it, but it does express the magnitude of realization. It is the end of you and the world and your whole way of looking at things. In this sense, it is like dying. To most people, this is also not a very attractive idea, but it does express the extent of transformation.

Consider all the usual ways you think about yourself and the world, and all the ways you make sense of and order these thoughts. Consider all the usual stories you tell yourself about who you are, what the universe is, how your life fits into it, the events of your youth, the events of ten years ago, and the events of last year, last week, and this morning. Imagine all of it suddenly evaporating like the disappearance of a mirage. You would not lose the memories, but your ego-self and your whole worldview would be revealed as a kind of dream from which you have awakened.

Despite teachings on the subject, there is a great tendency to think about enlightenment as gaining something, some new understanding or knowledge. But while the truth *can* be known, it cannot be known by the individual ego-self, not by the mind or body, which is what we tend to think we are. For the truth to be revealed, ego, mind, and body must fall away. The truth itself cannot be gained, for it is there all along. So nothing is acquired in awakening. It is more like losing everything, including yourself.

Again, this may not sound so great to the ego. If everything is lost, what will be left? This is a terrifying prospect for the ego, which will resist realization and create subtle tricks to maintain its delusions. It's important to stress this, though, so we don't make the mistake of thinking the path is a way of acquisition. Rather, we may know it as a way of letting go. Real progress on this path is not presaged by excitement over new ideas, or enthusiasm about practice. Instead, it is more indicated by genuine confusion, by exhaustion, by failure, by resignation, and above all, by disillusionment.

This may sound like a difficult and dismal path. And yes, we must pass through this darkness. Figuratively at least, we must bear the trials of renunciation and asceticism. We must shoulder our crosses and carry them to our doom. Don't make the mistake of thinking that because the ego is already unreal and we are already perfect as we are, that there is no point in making any effort toward realization. And lest you be discouraged from putting forth this effort, let us put the matter in a slightly different light.

Remember that grace is always present and at work in our lives. There is nothing greater than reality itself — the truth of what is — and our own realization is the greatest good we can achieve. Through awakening, we are liberated from suffering. We are freed from the grip of our thoughts and desires. We are enabled to act for the liberation of others. We are unbound from the chains of our hopes and fears. The delusions of the mind are dispelled. And in the absence of ignorance, the unending bliss of pure awareness is unveiled.

No Ego, No World, No Body, No Mind, No Thoughts

After awakening, one perceives no real separation, division, or distinction between subject and objects, between things and other things, between foreground and background, between inside and outside, between self and others, between self and world, between world and God. And so on. The reality of this is unimaginable beforehand, but afterward is clear to see.

The experience of awakening may include incredible relief, for all our problems are a function of the belief in these distinctions. It may include unimaginable joy and wondrous beauty, for that which is without separation is divinity itself, and the very space of consciousness radiates with bliss. It may include utter bewilderment, for the usual ways we make sense of the world are clearly unreal and no longer make sense. For example, the self cannot be located. There is not the usual feeling of being inside a body or mind. Nor is there the feeling of being outside of them.

When we look for the individual ego-self, that I-thought and the interior life that used to seem so real is fundamentally nowhere to be found. This could be very disorienting if one is not prepared in some way — or even if one is. The reality of selflessness is … well … more real than any conceptualization. We might wonder if we are insane, if we are experiencing the effects of a brain tumor, or even if we have died. In fact, all kinds of thoughts may arise, including thoughts like, *This is it!* or *I have attained enlightenment!* But there will be nowhere for these thoughts to stick, and nobody to believe in them. Like everything else, they will simply appear and disappear in the clarity of consciousness itself.

Although realization hits like a thunderbolt, complete, encompassing everything, the implications continue to unfold. Relatively speaking, the stream of thoughts has to play catch-up, struggling to articulate what has happened. Of course, it cannot — reality is beyond thoughts and words — but due to circumstances, it tries anyway.

One day it will be clear that the ego-self, the individual identity, is totally gone, and that it was always an illusion. One day it will be clear that not only is the ego an illusion, but so are the trees, the rocks, the sky, and the ground we walk upon. It is all as illusory as the ego. How can it be otherwise when there are no distinctions? And of course, it will be clear that the body too, like the rocks and trees and all things, is but a form appearing and disappearing in consciousness. But it doesn't stop there.

The reality behind all objects, all events, all patterns, all perceptions will be clear. One day it will be clear that the whole of the mind is an object that appears and disappears in the clarity of consciousness. One day, it will be clear that thoughts themselves, emotions, sensations, and impulses, like all objects and events, have no beginning and no end, no edge and no boundary.

For this one, then, there is no ego, no world, no body, no mind, no thought. And so on.

One will pass through ecstasy after ecstasy, and then at last will be at peace. One will reside in the heart, in the truth itself, in the limitless One.

ETERNAL PRESENCE

In the Hindu tradition, *Jnani* is a word for one who is Self-realized. *Jnana* means knowledge, and a jnani is the knower. The opposite of jnana, *ajnana*, is ignorance, which obscures direct knowledge of our true nature. That knowledge is reality itself, total perception, and the jnani is indistinguishable from it.

In the Hellenistic tradition, such a person is called a *gnostic*, a word signifying direct spiritual knowledge. *Buddha* is the name given to one who has awakened to such knowledge in the Buddhist tradition. The Christian tradition speaks of *perfection* or the *deified being,* one who is unified with God. The Muslim tradition speaks of *fana,* annihilation of the self, through which a person becomes aware of the unity of God with all things. In other traditions, this person might be called a shaman, a seer, or a prophet, and in some circumstances, a heretic, a fool, or a lunatic.

This is not to say that everyone so called has been enlightened. Most likely many have not. But these names can point to enlightenment, and I can say with no uncertainty that enlightened people have been and are among us. They are fully awake, teaching practices, guiding spiritual seekers, and pointing toward the truth. Although it could be said that they are not individual people anymore. For there is no such thing as personal enlightenment. Such a person is like the wind in the trees, like clouds passing in a clear blue sky, or like the sound of a mountain stream. They are nobody, really.

For those who do *not* know their true nature, the jnani appears as other individuals, as a person with a body going about and performing actions. Those who think they are their bodies and minds project the same situation onto the jnani. If this were the case, however, there would be no jnanis. Instead, for the jnani, there is nothing but reality itself. Body and mind, world and others, are all phenomena appearing and disappearing in the clarity of consciousness, and there is nothing but that. For the jnani, there is no individual self and there are no others. The source of all movements and actions, all thoughts, of all phenomena, is the source of everything — the limitless One. So really, there are not even separate movements or actions or thoughts to speak of.

That we are the pure being of reality itself is true for all. A jnani is simply that truth laid bare. In this sense, there is only one enlightenment, one knower, indistinguishable from the truth. Due to circumstances, each jnani may express this knowledge in different ways, but the appearance of all jnanis is simply the eternal presence of the unobstructed reality itself.

INEFFABLE BEING

It is natural to want to know about enlightenment. This pure desire is a manifestation of the very impulse that places us upon the spiritual path. It is natural to want to know what truth is, what it is like, but it is like nothing else. In fact, it is not really a *thing* at all. All things are limited and can be described through various distinctions. Reality itself — enlightenment — is indescribable because there are no limitations and no distinctions in it.

The fundamental duality that creates all distinctions between subject and object, foreground and background, inside and outside, past and future, and all paired opposites collapses into the divine reality. All dualities — all subjects, objects, worlds, and qualities — are revealed as manifestations of reality, but not reality itself, just as thoughts and dreams are a manifestations of consciousness, but not consciousness itself.

The world may appear, but it is only an image. This image is a manifestation of our true nature. But there is nothing beyond the horizon, or beneath the ground we walk on, and there is nothing behind our eyes except the divine reality. All things that arise are the manifestations of one supreme consciousness.

We could say, all internal activity appears as external manifestations. Or we could say, within and without are all within. For when we speak of totality, there can be no inside or outside, no unmanifested or manifested. So in all the known and unknown, there is nothing that is not known. The truth is always in plain sight. If hidden from us, it is we ourselves who have hidden it.

The desire to know the truth is the purest desire, and the only desire that can lead to lasting happiness. But because you are this truth, ignorance of it is nothing but ignorance itself. Drop this ignorance and the truth is there, as it always has been.

The intellect is completely dumbfounded. I'm trying to articulate the experience of clear seeing, of total perception. But it is a oneness so complete that the mind cannot grasp it, so all-encompassing that no doctrine, philosophy, or theology will do … unless it is to say something radically simple like, "There is nothing but God," or "Consciousness itself is all there is." But ultimately, this will not do either. It is beyond all concepts, all words, all thoughts. In the end, silence alone comes closest to speaking the truth.

When we drop the distractions of appearances, of objects and sounds, of the ego and its thoughts, of the body and its sensations, of the individual self and its emotions and preferences, its impulses and actions, when all attachments fall away, what is left but the wordless silence of being? This holy silence, this pure ineffable being, is the unending bliss of divine consciousness … and that is what we really are.

13

ABIDING IN TRUTH

Although the journey has a beginning and an end,
the truth has no beginning and no end.

CLEAR SEEING

Clear seeing is simply the total perception of unobstructed reality. Obstructions are the result of attachment to conscious or unconscious thoughts, such as: *I am my body, I am my mind, I am the thinker, I am the doer, I am separate from the world and others, I am these thoughts and memories,* and so on. Further obstructions result from belief in concepts and conceptual models, such as the material, mechanistic universe, or a transcendent reality apart from this one, or a hierarchy of divine beings, and so on.

Attachment to and belief in such thoughts are the sources of delusion, a kind of personal mirage that obscures the true nature of the self and reality. They are roadblocks to total perception.

These sticking points accumulate heaping tangles of interdependent thoughts. The result is an obstruction, which separates the subject of perception from the object of perception, be it a physical object, an emotion, a thought, or the entire universe.

When these obstructions are removed or rendered transparent, the whole circuit of perception is opened, and its unbroken, undivided nature is revealed. Subject and object collapse into the totality of perception, such that self perceives self and world perceives world. But really there is only the one being, manifesting as both self and world. The experience cannot be understood through the usual subject-object idea. In total perception, there is nowhere for the experience to rest. There is, essentially, no one who is having the experience.

This "nowhere for the experience to rest" is a deeper, esoteric meaning of the Gospel passage where Jesus responds to a scribe who pledges to follow him. He replies, "Foxes have dens and birds have nests, but the Son of Man has no place to lay his head." The usual interpretations talk about Jesus being homeless and the scribe being well off, so it's a way of saying there is a price to pay and you'll have to give up a lot. This may be so, but giving up wealth or material goods is only the external meaning. What one actually has to give up is much deeper than that. Look deeper and the whole of the teaching can be seen in the phrase "… the Son of Man has no place to lay his head."

Even if you have no interest in Christian scriptures or don't care for this interpretation, it could be noted that the mind is like the den of a fox, and the body is like the nest of a bird. When we identify with and become attached to the mind and to the body, we become like foxes and like birds. There, in the idea of the mind, in the idea of the body, we rest our heads. There we make our stand as separate individuals. There we make our home and establish our view. But ultimately, it is a mistaken view — or at least only a temporary one — based on identification and attachment. For in truth, there is nothing to hang on to. There is nowhere to rest our heads.

In awakening, this truth is ever-present. The cycle of identification has been broken. Attachments have fallen away. So whatever arises, be it of mind, body, or world, there is nowhere for the experience to rest. The impermanence and the relativity of all things is continuously recognized in each thing that arises, whatever it may be and whatever comes to pass. That is clear seeing.

In light of this, truly, profound surrender is our wondrous destiny!

LIVING TRUTH

Our lives are patterns within patterns within patterns — of thoughts, of energy, of sleeping and dreaming and waking, of emotions, of movement, of reactions and actions, of desires and behaviors, and so on. Ordinarily, we are caught up in these patterns through attachment and identification. We are caught up in the thoughts, and in the ideas, concepts, stories, individuals, objects, and worlds we fashion out of them.

The truth is always present, the reality in which all this appears. But caught in the appearances, hypnotized by them, we take the appearances for reality and think the truth is elsewhere. Eventually, we may begin our search for the truth, the great adventure of the spiritual journey. We look and look for this elusive truth. Sometimes we think we've found it, but when we look deeper it turns out to be wrong. Again and again we are disillusioned, until we are *completely* disillusioned.

When we have given up searching for the truth we think is elsewhere, then we may suddenly awaken to the living truth. We may suddenly realize its eternal presence. Of course, it has been there all along. Never for a moment have you been apart from it. It's like when you are looking everywhere for something you think you lost. You look everywhere but cannot find it. Then you finally give up, put your hand in your pocket, and there it is. It's been with you all along.

It is not even right to say that your ego is not it, or your body is not it. They *are* it, but so is everything else. Nothing is left out. Everything you imagine to be an impediment is actually a manifestation of your true being. But it is also beyond all things — beyond the ego, beyond the body, beyond the mind, beyond time and space, and so on.

So when we realize this truth ourselves, we transcend all things. This is not hyperbole. It does not mean that what we call the body, the mind, and the world do not appear at all. But all these things are transparent. The enlightened person sees all things as nothing but the divine reality, as nothing but the limitless One. The awakened one sees the living truth in all phenomena and in the absence of all phenomena. It is eternal, unbroken, and ever-present.

A Vast Unknowing

There is a well-known koan in which Bodhidharma, the founder of Zen and conveyor of Buddhism to China, meets the Emperor Wu. The Emperor was a great supporter of Buddhism and had built many temples and monasteries. Upon meeting what appeared to be a holy man from India, he asks what merit all this support will grant him.

Bodhidharma replies, "No merit whatsoever."

Taken aback, the Emperor asks, "But what is the ultimate teaching then?"

Bodhidharma replies, "Vast emptiness, nothing holy."

Again, disturbed by the man's replies, the Emperor asks, "Who are you, who comes before me?"

Bodhidharma replies, "I don't know."

Here would be an opportune time for the Emperor to realize enlightenment, or at least have a moment of clarification or release. Unfortunately, the Emperor doesn't really get it. So Bodhidharma goes away, sets up shop in a cave and stares at a wall for nine years.

After Bodhidharma has left, it is suggested to the Emperor that the man was none other than the embodiment of compassion, but the Emperor still doesn't get it.

What is there to get, except "Vast emptiness, nothing holy," and "I don't know"? If we get this, we get nothing. Having nothing, we realize everything.

The truth is without any limits whatsoever. Without limits, nothing can be grasped. All thoughts, all ideas, all concepts, all models are empty, collapsing even as they arise. There is absolutely nothing to hold on to. There is no merit to be gained. And yet, how wonderful! This vast unknowing is liberation itself.

THE BLISS OF BEING

Many who start out upon the spiritual path begin with a search for their idea of happiness or a search for ecstatic or blissful states. Like drug users, we seek some kind of high, some kind of wonderful experience. But whatever happens, whatever happiness we achieve, whatever states we go into, whatever experiences we have, they do not last. For all ideas, all states, all experiences are impermanent. If we experience a high, then we will eventually come down. Based on such experiences, then, it is difficult if not impossible to imagine the nature of all-pervasive bliss.

Be clear in this. Whatever is not always present, in every possible state, in every possible experience — in short, whatever is not always here and now — cannot be all pervasive. Therefore, it cannot be the ultimate truth or reality. Whatever arises passes away. We can verify this through our experience. The way of all things is impermanence, to arise and subside, to appear and disappear.

So the truth of enlightenment cannot be anything new. It is already present. All that is needed is to remove obscuring thoughts. Do not think the truth is elsewhere or that divinity is far off. Do not think that happiness is in the future or that liberation is to be gained. Do not think yourself worthy or unworthy. Do not think awakening is something that arises or will arise. Enlightenment is always here and now. It is always within the present experience. It never leaves anything out. That is the great joy of awakening. Even "obscuring thoughts" cannot obscure the light of its presence.

There is a happiness that does not rely on ideas, on particular states, or on any condition or experience. It is there in the depths of grief and in the throes of pain. It is there in hunger and longing and restlessness. It is there in sadness and confusion. It is there in triumph and defeat, joy and sorrow, hope and despair. It is there in ecstasy and in misery. It is there in waking, in dreaming, and in deep sleep. It is there in the mind and there out of the mind. It is there in the body and there out of the body. It is there before birth and there after death.

So our spiritual journey must take us from a search for a false happiness of transient thoughts and states, to the true happiness which transcends all thoughts and states. For although this true happiness is present through it all, through all the ups and downs, awakening to its presence is the end of suffering. When all thoughts, all ideas, all concepts, all states, all objects, all experiences, and so on are made transparent through awakening, our true nature is revealed as the one reality, as pure being. This pure being is awareness itself. And this awareness is all-pervasive bliss.

Choiceless Action

Reality itself requires no measure of belief, no philosophy, no doctrine, no ideology. It is, by definition, what is. People may debate what is happening. Some will believe one thing, while others believe another thing. But whether we feel confused or not, and no matter where we are on the spiritual path, there should be no difficulty in admitting that whatever is happening must be an aspect or manifestation of a fundamental reality.

That awareness exists is undeniable. After that, we go into all our various conditioned thoughts, ideas, assumptions, concepts, and conceptual experiences. In short, we are caught up in our delusions about who we are and what is happening. Without our conditioned thoughts, beyond this fundamental awareness, what can we say? We tend to think "getting it" will be something complicated, some explanation or constructed model of an ordered reality. But our attempts to grasp at it are always a type of speculation only. In our speculation we lose sight of reality itself, which is always within our immediate awareness.

We should consider this deeply. What's happening now is always what's really happening. Whatever arises … that is what's happening. That is reality. But all our ideas about it do not lead to seeing clearly. That is the noise of delusion, and the source of ignorance and confusion. So when there is awareness, there is awareness. When thoughts appear, thoughts appear. When sensations are felt, sensations are felt. When images are seen, images are seen. When actions take place, actions take place. This is how awareness is and how all things happen. What is there to be confused about?

Ordinarily, we keep ourselves in reserve, as separate beings, positing the individual self as an interactor with reality, rather than something arising within reality itself. By keeping this individual self separate, we make room for all our thoughts and ideas, for time and space, for inside and outside, for all our speculations and delusions. We make room for our suffering, our unhappiness, and our hopes for things to be different than they are.

Enlightenment is not complicated. It just doesn't leave anything out. All things are included within the one reality, including the individual self. So when the ego appears, the ego appears. That's all. When it disappears, it disappears, just like everything else appearing and disappearing in the clarity of consciousness. When this is the case, everything is taken care of. All action is choiceless action.

At any given moment, whatever is happening is what's happening. There is no way what is happening could be any other way. And that will always be the case, no matter what you do. Because it will always be now. In our delusion we may find this disturbing, as if we are like robots, bound to a destiny beyond our control. But that's because we are holding ourselves in reserve as separate beings. Include yourself, as you are, in the picture, and there are no conflicts whatsoever. Everything is freely unfolding exactly as it is unfolding.

Although we may make many mistakes as individuals, and we put forth effort on the spiritual journey, this is only from the individual point of view. Our true nature is always free and effortless. It never makes mistakes. Trust in this higher power and there is nothing to worry about. Just surrender and allow compassion to do its work.

14

FREEDOM AND POWER

True freedom and power only appear
when we stop grasping at all their illusory forms.

EFFORTLESS ACCOMPLISHMENT

We set out upon the journey fully identified with the individual self, with the ego, mind, and body. We hold an idea that we are the thinker of thoughts, the feeler of sensations and emotions, and the doer of actions. This idea determines our conceptual experience. In this guise, any progress we make on the journey and any accomplishments we achieve in life happens according to our efforts. That is the situation.

Effort is unavoidable as long as these ideas hold and the cycle of identification continues. Whatever we do — even if we do nothing — it is essentially through effort as long as we believe we are the doer, the source of effort. We cannot escape it by doing nothing, because we will still think we are the doer of nothing.

If one speaks of bondage, this is how we are bound, constrained to our ideas about who and what we are, and to our conceptual experience. Because it's not the truth — not really what's happening — we are subject to suffering, frustration, and so on. Because we are deluded, we are subject to wrong views, to selfishness, to evil, and so on.

We imagine that as individuals we have the power to choose or choose differently in the future, to decide upon one action over another action, to make an effort or not to make it. We imagine the same about the past, that somehow we could have chosen differently than we did. But these illusions only hold so long as we are projecting ourselves into an imaginary future and an imaginary past. What's happening now is always what's really happening, and it cannot be otherwise.

The question to ask is not, how can we make the right choices, but who is projecting this choice. What is the origin of the whole situation? What is really happening? The question is not, what will happen or what could have happened if such and such, but what is really happening right now.

When we realize and awaken to the eternal now, everything is revealed as free and effortless. But it is not free because of the choice we thought we had. It is free precisely because it is what really is and cannot be otherwise. Because it is choiceless, it is absolutely free. And it is not effortless because the individual self has acquired supreme power. It is the opposite. The individual self has lost all its illusions of power, lost itself even. It is effortless because the true power is revealed, that which already makes all things appear and disappear — that which moves all, does all, sees all, is all.

So for the awakened one, whatever they may seem to do, there is no individual to claim it or take credit. Whatever they may seem to accomplish, it is accomplished effortlessly. It is like leaves falling, like waves spreading across the water, like wind blowing through a canyon. Even if they appear to work, they work without working. Even if they appear to struggle, they struggle without struggling. They may teach. They may continue various activities. But for them, there is nothing to be gained or lost, no success or failure, for they have already realized the truth. There is nothing missing and not a single thing out of place.

Consciousness Without Limits

Picture a beautiful lake surrounded by tall trees. We are sitting on a dock looking out across the water. A wind blows down through the trees and creates ripples on the surface. The sun shines, turning the ripples into shifting patterns of light and shadow, all across the lake.

Transfixed, we are hypnotized by the busy, active surface of the lake, by undulating shadows and glittering sparkles of light. Eventually, the wind dies down. The surface of the lake becomes calm … smooth … perfectly still. Suddenly, instead of the play of light and shadow on the surface of the lake, reflected there are the sun itself, the trees, the blue sky, the clouds, the birds, and ourselves, too. The entire world is reflected in the surface of the lake.

We can imagine life's journey like this. We think we are experiencing one thing, but what is actually being experienced is something very different.

The seeking mind is quite busy. It is active and at the same time transfixed by its own activity. Furthermore, because we are identified with the mind and believe it to be the source of our thoughts and behavior, we imagine this activity to be the key to our search. If we could just get rid of all this activity and have a clear mind. But whenever we catch a glimpse of a clear mind, we attribute it to mind and try to find it again through mind activity.

We may think, *If I could just maintain mindful awareness, then I could master my thoughts and behavior.* But the mind we imagine, which is mind as ego, comes and goes all the time. When we pay attention to it, there it is. When we are distracted, it is nowhere to be seen. When we wake up in the morning, it appears. When we go to sleep, it disappears.

We cannot fix this transient mind. When we attempt to do so, we are merely confused about the goal of our practice. In reality, there is no such mind. It is only an object appearing in the clarity of consciousness. It is only a dance of light and shadow. We may think we are seeking the still reflection of the whole world, but it too is a play of light and shadow.

To keep this analogy going, what we really seek is what has been there all along: the surface of the lake itself … and its depths.

This is why, for the awakened one, active mind or quiet mind makes no difference. For that one, there is no mind. There is only the unbroken clarity of consciousness itself. Everything is that, be it undulating shadows and glittering lights, or the whole world. And when all these things disappear, it still remains. Of course, all analogies breaks down, for in truth there is no stopping point for the awakened one's experience. Consciousness moves freely as total perception. The sun itself and the lake are one. There is no boundary, no limit, no beginning, no end.

Responsive Behavior

While identified with mind and body, we feel that the individual ego-self is the source and director of our behavior and activity. And yet, so often we cannot seem to get a handle on ourselves. We repeat the same patterns of conditioned thoughts and behaviors again and again. If we try to change ourselves, we fight with ourselves. And we are left to wonder, are there two selves, that one can argue with another?

In this egoic mode of being, we constantly struggle for control, as if our lives were a battle for ego-territory. Whatever we can claim as under our control we see as victory, and what is beyond our control we see as suspect at best, and defeat at worst. And yet, as egos, we cannot control the reflexive behaviors of our own bodies, and we cannot control the conditioned thoughts of our own minds. No wonder we experience suffering!

To make the point very clear: we suffer because of our own delusions, because of ignorance. We suffer because our ideas about what is happening and how things work are not what is actually happening and not how things actually work. So at every point where there is some discrepancy between our ideas of reality and reality itself, the ego suffers. This suffering is actually a wakeup call, but instead of heeding the call, the ego will double down. As a reflex action, the ego will patch up ideas, invent new concepts, shuffle around old ones, shift around its identity, and basically do anything to keep itself as the center of attention.

So when suffering arises, if we follow our conditioned thoughts and reflexes, we perpetuate our ignorance. We renew the cycle of identification and restoke the fires of delusion. But if we hear the wakeup call and step out upon the path, if we seek with sincerity the root of all suffering, then awakening is near.

For the awakened one, the mind and body, the individual ego-self are just ideas themselves. They are objects that arise and subside in the clarity of consciousness. They cannot be the source and director of our activity and behavior, for they are nothing but activity and behavior themselves. For the awakened one, the source of everything is the source of everything. It can be no other.

Thus thoughts, intentions, behaviors, and actions all arise naturally, in harmony with the present circumstances. Everything is responsive to the total environment. There is no question of control or lack of control. There is no battle for territory, no victory or defeat, and alas … no suffering.

Everyday Simplicity

All our lives, it seems, we are seeking something special that is elsewhere. As children we might imagine it is special to be an adult, to go on adventures, to get married, to have kids, and so on. But as adults we are rarely satisfied with our situation or attainments. We continue seeking, for a perfect partner, a peak experience, a feeling of success or accomplishment. And in our spiritual lives — which is really just our whole lives — we are also seeking something special that we imagine is elsewhere.

We may have many ideas about the goal of the spiritual journey. Surely it must be something special and far off. It must be difficult to reach, and yet it promises to fulfill all our wishes for happiness and satisfaction. Having found it, we will command an understanding of the universe and be empowered to explain it to others. We will attain inner peace and clarity.

Relatively speaking, such thoughts contain elements of truth, but they are seen through deep-rooted egoic delusions. Much effort can be expended trying to move forward, but if we are pointed in the wrong direction, our efforts will be counterproductive. So for the sake of clarity, let us try to state simply some fundamental misunderstandings. I'm not saying they will immediately make sense — that's why they are misunderstandings — but as we come toward the end here, we will at least be pointing in the right direction.

Foremost among misunderstandings is misidentification, the thought that we are the mind-body, the individual ego-self. As long as we imagine that this separate ego can attain enlightenment or experience its fruits, we will remain in ignorance of our true nature.

The second misunderstanding is that of remoteness, that enlightenment must be far off and in the future. This has its roots in misidentification. The ego-self is projected into space and time. It always imagines awakening to be somewhere else, for someone else, or far off in the future. As long as we project the ego-self in space and time, we will not recognize the here and now, where the reality of enlightenment is always present.

The third misunderstanding is that of specialness, that the enlightened state is an extraordinary state. This too has its roots in misidentification, for it relates to the thought that the ego will attain enlightenment. Certainly awakening is extraordinary from the point of view that our delusion and suffering are ordinary. Nothing can describe the joy and relief of realization. But enlightenment reveals what is ever present as our true nature. So in this sense, we could say it is totally ordinary.

For the awakened one, however, there is neither the ordinary nor the extraordinary. Everything is seen as the limitless One. Everything is present, here and now. So there is nothing to seek. This present moment is always perfect, always complete. Nothing is ever left out. So this everyday simplicity, just going about one's business, this ordinary being, is already divine.

Invincible Peace

We can point toward enlightenment by trying to say what it isn't and what it is. But know that it is actually beyond all words, all thoughts, all concepts. For the awakened one, there is no ignorance or enlightenment, no bondage or freedom, no limitation or power. That is true enlightenment, true freedom, and true power.

When we say, there is absolutely nothing to hang on to, nothing that can be grasped, no safety in any attachment ... that can be disturbing, even terrifying. The ego-self is itself a thing we hang on to, formed through grasping, and it always seeks safety through various attachments. To say our true nature has no boundary and is totally without limits can also be troubling, even horrifying. Even the notion of all-pervasive bliss may sound scary, for we sense, deep down, we will have to let go of ourselves to realize it.

Actually, we will have to let go of everything — not just the ego-self, but the world as well. Until then, subjects and objects will continue to arise, and there is constant struggle.

But wherever you are on your journey, do not fear to tread the path. In truth you are already on it. Do not let your doubts dissuade you from your quest. Find out for yourself who you really are and what enlightenment is. Awaken from your egoic dream, and recognize your true nature as the limitless One.

For when realization dawns, when there really is nothing to hang on to anymore, all your doubts will be assuaged. You will weep with joy. You will laugh with relief. Nothing being apart from you, there will be nothing to fear. All things being transparent, there will be nobody to be troubled. Without a past or future, you will dwell in eternity. And within that, within you already, is this invincible peace.

APPENDIX A

More Short Answers about Enlightenment

In the previous book, I included some short answers about enlightenment taken from questions I have received. Since I continue to receive questions, I will include a few more answers here. Although drawn from actual questions, they are all treated in the abstract, and do not pertain to particular people or situations. I've tried to write concise answers to some difficult questions. Of course, much more could be said on these topics ... or nothing at all. Silence itself actually comes closest to the truth.

Q: What is enlightenment?

A: It is nothing you can attain and nothing that you lack, but it is real liberation from the delusion that you lack it or have attained it. In a way, you are already there, for you *are* that which you seek. It is before you now. You may not know it yet, but a revelation comes in which all this is completely realized. Both the seeker and the sought after fall away. Then, all separation dissolves into the one Reality. That is true being, unadorned consciousness, and all-pervasive bliss.

Q: Can a liberated person exhibit fear, experience pain, or act as if they have a preference for something over something else, such as avoiding pain or death?

A: To view true freedom as being free *from* something is the wrong way of looking at things. That kind of freedom only exists through separation of self and world. It is a false freedom. Through separation, one imagines that when liberated they will be free from conditioning, the body, and the mind. But actual liberation is without separation entirely. There is no conditioning, no body, and no mind to be free from. True freedom is to never be in conflict with what is and how things are, whatever may arise. There is only the limitless One, and all phenomena, be it fear or pain or preference, are nothing but the One. A similar mistake is made if one thinks liberation is a kind of mind state. If one's body or mind had to be a certain way, one would not really be free. For whatever arises, passes away. True freedom is eternal. It is to always be as you are.

Q: Can someone exhibiting bad behavior be enlightened?

A: To think that such matters can be settled in the mind is the path of delusion. Bad behavior is bad behavior. Enlightenment is enlightenment. When the truth appears, bad behavior vanishes and there are no others to discuss. When the truth vanishes, bad behavior appears in yourself and others. Nevertheless, there are those who suffer from bad behavior, and those who are liberated from it. Some who speak of enlightenment are not, and some who do not speak of it, are. It is most helpful for everyone if we tend to the situation at hand, whatever it may be. Compassion never discriminates. It is like thousands of things being done at once, and yet, nobody is doing it.

Q: Why is it so hard to make spiritual progress?
A: Who says it is difficult? Every day God delivers priceless treasure at our feet. But so often we don't even notice, even when day after day such treasure is delivered. Maybe we notice something, but too often we say it's not good enough, and wait for something better. There is nothing better than God's treasure! Don't be silly. Whatever it is, accept it!

Q: What is the most direct path to realization?
A: To realize now! Anything other than that is indirect. There are approaches through the mind, through the body, through objects, through religions, through dreams, and so on. What makes any one path less indirect than another is really according to each person's outlook and background. That is why so many paths are available. But whatever the path, the fundamental issue of identification with mind, body, and ego must be addressed. So the expedient path for any individual is the one that gets to this issue most directly.

Q: Can enlightenment be lost?
A: Whatever can be gained can be lost. But enlightenment is not a matter acquisition. It cannot be gained or lost. Even now, Reality is present for everyone. It is only ignorance that

obscures realization. God is the eternal, limitless One. When all things are revealed to be nothing but that, what can ever be gained or lost?

Q: Why do some people seem to sink back into delusion after an experience of awakening?

A: If awakening is not complete, something remains separate, and whatever that is draws the person back into delusion. Such an experience is highly significant, but the person may still be holding on to the individual self, the mind or the body, or may still be holding on to external objects, others, or the world. For complete awakening, nothing can be left out or remain separate. Everything must be surrendered. If so much as an atom, a thought, or an idea is held back, the delusions of dualistic viewpoints will return. Strictly speaking, it is not a fault in the person. It is just what's happening. One could say, it is their karma or their destiny. Through grace they have been granted great insight, but they have not yet completed the journey.

Q: How will I know if I am deceiving myself?

A: Here's how you can know if you are deceiving yourself. Ask yourself, *Is it a thought?* If the answer is yes, then you are deceiving yourself. That may seem radical, but the truth is radical just like that. It is beyond all thoughts.

Q: I see the idea of awakening appearing more and more in popular culture. Is this because more and more people are waking up?

A: It's possible, but you see it more due to your outlook. Such stories have been around for thousands of years. They appear because they are written into the fabric of our being, because deep down, we cannot escape our true nature. So the quest to find it and the awakening to it are reflected in the stories we tell. Self realization is at the heart of all stories, and so is reflected in them all to varying degrees. The more aware you are of your own journey, the more you will see it reflected in stories.

Q: Couldn't consciousness itself also be an illusion?

A: Don't be confused by words. Of course, when viewed as a concept, consciousness itself is also an illusion. In other words, if you think consciousness is anything other than the one Reality, then of course it is an illusion. The one Reality is the one Reality, whether it is called the one Reality, Tao, God, Buddha, or Material. Because of the ideas people hold, sometimes it is useful to call it consciousness itself. In any case, it is only revealed by realization, not by a word or a concept. It is beyond all words and concepts.

Q: What's the point really?

A: What is it that you are really looking for? Ask yourself that. Aside from real happiness and an end to suffering, need there be any other point? The truth is not practical in the way a hat is. Nor is it valuable in the way gold is, or beautiful in the way a landscape is. It is beyond practical, beyond valuable, beyond beautiful. For it is that in which all these have their being. But

I ask you, what could be more practical, more valuable, more beautiful than recognition of the truth?

Q: Seriously, how can you be sure about all this stuff?

A: The question reveals a mind still trapped in the thought that one will grasp things as being a certain way. The truth is not like that. It has no thoughts attached to it. It is simply what is. Anything I say is merely an attempt to point, to encourage inquiry, or to shock the mind into suddenly casting off all concepts, all thoughts, all delusions. When that happens, recognition of the ineffable will be as clear to you as an image of your own face. Can you deny that your face is your face? Well … it's kind of like that.

ABOUT THE AUTHOR

On April 11th, 2016 Matthew Lowes had an unexpected and profound spiritual awakening, just as the great mystics have described. Since this enlightenment dawned, he has endeavored to communicate the insights intrinsic to realization and help others on their spiritual journey. In addition to this work, he continues to be a writer of fiction and games, as well as a student and teacher of martial arts, fitness, and health practices.

matthewlowes.com

Without the mind, there is no confusion whatsoever.

A BILLION FINGERS POINT AT THE MOON

MATTHEW LOWES

DECIPHERING SPIRITUAL LANGUAGE

Deconstruct the confusion inherent in the language of
spirituality, and orient yourself toward a truth which is
beyond all words, thoughts, and concepts.

—Coming in 2022

Thank you for reading!

Please post a review online. :)

The next book in this series,
A Billion Fingers Point at the Moon,
is coming in 2022.